RETIREMENT SUCCESS IS
IN YOUR HANDS!

Dave Hall

I hope you enjoy reading my book as much as I enjoyed writing it!

It would mean the world to me if you would consider leaving a review on Amazon to let me know what you think of the book.

So, if you have a few minutes to spare after you read, you can search for the book on Amazon, scroll to the bottom and look for "Review This Product" and then click on "write a customer review." Even a quick review will go a long way!

Your review helps not only me as an author, but gets word out about my new book, too!

- Dave Hall, CPA

GETTING

SAFELY

THROUGH

RETIREMENT

A NEW PARADIGM IN RETIREMENT PLANNING

DAVE HALL, CPA

Getting Safely Through Retirement

Copyright @2023 by Dave Hall, CPA

Available Online at:

www.gettingsafelythroughretirement.com

———————————————————————————

Library of Congress Cataloging Data

Getting Safely Through Retirement / Dave Hall, CPA

ISBN: 979-8-218-19012-5

Business / Finance

———————————————————————————

To maintain the anonymity of those, if any, involved, I have changed some details and names.

Some sample scenarios in this book are fictitious. Any similarity to actual persons, living or dead, is coincidental.

This book is educational and factual content regarding retirement planning. It may be used as guidance but is not meant to substitute a financial professional.

Printed in the United States of America.

To my beautiful wife
for being by my side.

and

My eight kids
for being my inspiration.

CONTENTS

CHAPTER 1 – AMERICA HAS A RETIREMENT PROBLEM

CHAPTER 2 – HAVE RETIREMENT PLANS ALWAYS BEEN SUBJECT TO ALL THESE RISKS?

CHAPTER 3 – RISK #1: SOCIAL SECURITY RISK

CHAPTER 4 – RISK #2: TAX RATE RISK

CHAPTER 14 – 5 STRATEGIES TO A RISK-FREE RETIREMENT

CHAPTER 15 – WHAT DO I DO NEXT?

CASE STUDY - CARLOS AND MARIA GARCIA

Preface

I was sitting in a Las Vegas church one sunny spring afternoon in the early 2000s when one of our youth leaders announced the details of our annual fathers and sons overnighter. I had been raised attending these annual overnighters with my own dad and brothers when I lived in Southern Utah. I had not attended one since I moved to Las Vegas because I did not have a son who was old enough to take with me. But this year was different. My oldest son Todd was now four years old. He was very mobile, and had proven he was okay to be away from his mother for a day or two.

The plan for the campout was to travel to the foothills east of Interstate 15 between Las Vegas, Nevada, and the California border just before Primm. Although these foothills are at a higher elevation than the Las Vegas valley, the terrain is still desert with very little shade. There was a location at the base of the foothills where we could park our cars for the night. From the parking area we would take our backpacks and hike what this leader estimated to be about one mile to the campsite. Once we got to the campsite we would cook dinner, play some games, eat s'mores, tell some stories, sleep, have breakfast, and return home mid-morning the next day.

This all seemed easy enough. I was in my early 30s, and I was in decent shape. I believed Todd was old enough to be able to walk the estimated mile it would require to get to camp. But if he could not, it wouldn't be a big deal. I would just carry him with our pack, and we would have no problem making it the expected distance to the campsite.

The day finally arrived for the campout. It was in the middle of May and the weather was unseasonably hot. Knowing this, I included with my gear extra water for Todd and me to have for the trip. We kissed my wife and Todd's little sister Alisha good-bye and drove out to the planned location. Because of everyone's differing work schedules there had not been a set time to meet at the parking area. When we got there, we saw a few other cars belonging to members of our church which confirmed we were in the right place.

Todd and I unpacked our gear from the car and headed out. Everything went very smooth for the first half mile. Todd was walking fine with minimal stops. As we got into the second half mile, Todd started to get tired, and we both started to consume more water than we had expected due to the extreme heat. As we approached what I estimated to be about a mile from where we had started our trek, Todd announced he could not walk anymore and needed to rest. As we were resting, a few other guys from our church passed us with their older sons. We had brief conversations with each of them, expecting we would soon be at the campsite together where we could talk more.

After resting for about 15 minutes, I put my pack back onto my back, lifted Todd up into my arms and started to walk. After about another mile of on-again-off-again walking I was shocked to realize I still could not see the campsite. I lowered Todd from my arms, and we sat down again to rest. By this point we were approaching the halfway mark on the water we had brought. I had assumed we'd have been to camp over a mile ago, so I had not been prepared for this extra hiking in the desert.

I finally got enough energy to get up and we continued to walk (it was primarily me walking by this point because Todd was so tired). We hiked another mile without seeing any sign of the camp. By this point I was not only exhausted, but I was starting to get scared. We were now down to about a quart of water, the camp was nowhere in sight, and Todd and I were still thirsty. I did not know what to do. I had not seen any forks in the road, so I assumed we had to still be on the right path, but now I was in a mess. I did not have enough water or energy left to get both Todd and me back out. I also did not have enough water to go forward and believe we could make it back out safely the next morning either.

I finally decided I just had to keep moving forward and hope I could make it to camp where someone could help me. As I did, I worried, I stressed, and I prayed. This is the last place I ever thought I would find myself. I had seen stories on the news about this type of thing happening to people, but I never expected it to happen to me. After about another half mile of walking and at the point of complete exhaustion from having to carry a 40-pound backpack and Todd, I finally saw the camp.

Todd and I shuffled into camp looking like we had just gotten out of a swimming pool due to the sweat pouring off our bodies. I must admit, I was extremely excited to know we had made it, but I was still genuinely concerned about how we were going to make it back home the next morning. We were safe for now, but there was no way we had enough water to get back out to our car. Luckily, there were other guys who were better prepared than I was, and they agreed to share their extra water with us. Plus, the individual who organized the event agreed to do what he could to help us since he felt bad for giving me inaccurate information on how far the camp really was.

As I have thought back on this event over the years and what I do as a retirement risk advisor, I have found so many similarities in what I experienced that day in the desert and what many of you are going to experience during your retirement. Many of you have scrimped for years, saved diligently and invested wisely throughout your life to prepare yourself for retirement. But there are several risks you have not contemplated that are going to cause a lot of concern. For some of you, your trip through retirement is going to be much like my trip through the desert. You have estimated how long your retirement journey will be and have set aside the money you believe you will need to get through this period, but you will live much longer than you had originally planned. You will also have setbacks along the way because the road will be filled with risks you had not anticipated.

The purpose of this book is to teach those of you who are still getting ready for retirement, as well as those of you who are already in retirement, about the Top 10 Financial Risks Facing Your Retirement. And since nobody wants to just focus on their problems, this book also includes solutions and strategies. These solutions and strategies can be used to reduce or even eliminate each of these risks, so you can take the worry out of your retirement. Your retirement should be a time you get to enjoy the benefits of your hard work. It should be a time to reflect on all the good things you have going on with your life and family. It should also be a time to pursue the opportunities you have waiting for you as a retiree – not worrying about whether you are going to run out of money before you run out of retirement and die broke.

My Story

I was raised in a small farming community in Southern Utah in the 1970s and -80s. My family consisted of my mom, my dad, me, my two older brothers, and my three older sisters. During my early years I spent a lot of time out of the house with my friends. Most of our outings consisted of simple activities like hikes in the hills, building forts we could hide and play in, playing under the streetlight, catching snakes and small animals we could turn into pets, and lots and lots of sports. My friends and I went to the same school. We attended the same church every Sunday, we played in the same sports leagues, and we bought our candy from the same corner store. As much as it seemed like we were all the same, there was one thing that caused a stark difference in the way I lived compared to the way my friends lived. The difference was what our dads did for work. My friends' dads were all successful farmers, business owners or teachers, but not my dad. My dad was a laborer for the Union Pacific Railroad. And unlike the jobs my friends' dads had, my dad's job never brought in enough money to cover all the financial needs a family our size had. This difference in economics started to create a lot of jealousy in me towards my friends and their families. I realized their financial situation bought them much more freedom than I had. Unlike me, my friends did not have to wait for their dad's paycheck to show up to be able to buy all the things they needed. When my friends went shopping, they were not stuck buying off-brand clothes like I was. They were able to buy name brand clothes and supplies. My friends and their families also went on trips and attended activities my family just couldn't afford.

This consistent financial struggle was real and the stress it put on my family seemed too much to bear at times. To overcome the lack of income from my dad's job, my mom did her part to help supplement his income even though her main job was a stay-at-home mom. She always ran a very tight budget. She was the master tailor for most of our school clothes. She managed a garden and farm animals that provided most of the food we would eat, and she worked long hours during harvest time when the farmers needed temporary workers. Everything my mom did helped, but it was never quite enough to make up for the lack of income created by the size of my dad's paycheck.

Then, when I was about 12, things went from bad to worse for my family. My mom found out she had breast cancer. I was devastated. At this age my mom was my everything. Over the years we had built a very close relationship through the endless hours we had spent together working with the crops and the farm animals. Most of my siblings hated the work so they would do everything they could to get out of it, often leaving my mom and I to do the work by ourselves. This time became very special to me because it gave me the opportunity to talk to my mom about life and listen to her advice.

After my mother's cancer diagnosis, our family dynamics changed. There were no cancer treatment facilities in Southern

Utah where we lived, so my mom had to move in with relatives in Northern Utah to get the help she needed. My dad's job required him to work away from home at the time. This meant my siblings and I had to move in with an aunt and uncle and their family just so we could have someone to take care of us.

After months of treatment and a miracle from God, my mom survived her cancer, and she was able to come back home. But our financial situation immediately changed for the worse. Any extra money that might have been available before my mom's cancer was now gone. My parents now sent every extra dollar we had each month to medical companies to cover unpaid bills from my mother's treatment.

It was at this time in my life that I first began to realize that not only were we poor, but my family had major financial issues, and the frustration I was experiencing because of our situation started to grow. Due to the financial burden placed on my family from the unpaid medical bills, my mom started having us kids do things we had never done before. She arranged for us kids to wash dishes at the school during lunch time to cover the cost of the lunch the school was providing since my parents could no longer afford to pay for it. All extracurricular activities we were a part of that required money came to a complete halt. All projects around the house that my friends' families were paying others to do for them we were doing ourselves. Including spending weeks digging a new sewer trench the city required us to have in order to switch from the septic tank system we had been using to a city sewer system. In order to connect to our downstairs bathroom the trench had to be 9 feet deep, about 3 feet wide, and 150 feet long. We did not have the $1,500 my friends' families were paying to have the trench dug with a backhoe, so we did it all by hand with buckets and shovels.

Our financial situation got so bad my mom even changed the way she approached my dad's paycheck. My dad's paycheck came in the mail every two weeks (I know, it is hard to believe, but employees have not always been able to have their paychecks directly deposited into their bank account). Prior to having cancer, my mom would pick these checks up from the post office on an inconsistent basis as she was out running errands for the family. Since her cancer, my mom was now making me or one of my siblings bike the mile to the post office every day, regardless of the weather, starting about three days before my dad was supposed to receive his paycheck up until his paycheck came. Her hope was that the check would come early, which it sometimes did, so she could get a head start on covering the unpaid medical bills and costs associated with daily living.

This paycheck-to-paycheck lifestyle had a significant impact on me. It frustrated me not only for myself, but also because I hated seeing my parents worry, stress themselves out, and sometimes even fight because of their lack of money. I hated seeing the sadness in my mother's eyes when she had to tell me or one of my siblings that we could not do what our friends were doing because we just could not afford it.

It was during this time of frustration and jealousy I made a commitment to myself that would ultimately change my life forever. "Dave," I said, I couldn't think of a better name to call myself, "when you leave this house and get married you are not going to require your family to live this way." I didn't know a lot about life then, but I did know I did not want my future family living under the stress my family was living under. And I was willing to do whatever it took to keep this from happening.

It was not long after this original commitment to myself that I made a second commitment, which was that I was going to go to college and become an accountant. I know a future in accounting probably does not sound like a very exciting goal to you, but I was good at math and as a poor boy, who was raised out in the country on a small farm, it was about the only thing I had that I could turn into an opportunity.

I wish I could tell you my parents' financial stress ended when I left the house at age 18, but it did not. My parents were never able to put money into an IRA or 401(k). The only place they ever traveled was to Northern Utah or Southern Nevada because we had relatives in both places they could stay with. The cars they bought were usually on their last leg. If the house needed repairs, they continued to fix it themselves, if they could. If they couldn't, they hired a professional and then got a loan so they could pay for the costs of the repair over time.

My parents both died having never experienced what it feels like to be financially secure. My mom passed away at age 60 never having had more than a few thousand dollars to her name. My dad passed away at 72 having slightly more money, but it was only because the government provided him with a $50,000 death benefit on my mom's life out of the Downwinders Fund. This fund had been set up for those who had cancer during their lifetime due to the radiation they were exposed to from the atomic bomb testing that took place during the early 1950s in the deserts of Southern Nevada. The radiation clouds from the testing blew over Southern Utah as a result many of my family members, including my mom, died too young. It was not uncommon for her generation to spend hours outside watching these big orange clouds blow over the city, not realizing the long-term impact it would have on their health.

As a kid it was easy to get caught up in all the things my family did not have. As I've gotten older, I have come to realize there is something my parents had that even some of my friend's parents did not. My parents had a never-ending love and commitment to my siblings and me that I will forever be grateful for. This love has not only helped me become the person I am today, but it also gave me the determination to keep the commitments I had made to myself when I was younger.

I became the only person in my family to ever graduate from college. I married my beautiful wife Lisa while attending college in Cedar City, Utah, and we now have eight children. I put in the work to become a successful certified public accountant (CPA). But the best part is I learned what it takes to put together a risk-based retirement plan so I can do for you what I could never do for my parents: teach what it takes to get safely through retirement.

In life some of our greatest blessings come from our greatest challenges. Had I not gone through what I did as a child, there is no way I would have put forth the sweat, financial loss, and tears required to become an expert in risk-based retirement planning. I would have given up years and thousands of dollars ago, accepting the fact that retirement was never going to be what I believed it could be.

Your story is going to be different from my story, and it is okay. Some of you will have been raised in a home where you never wanted for anything, and others will have been raised in a home where there was endless need beyond what even I experienced. But one thing is for certain: financial stress is real, and you need to do everything you can to eliminate the worry it can cause in your retirement.

CHAPTER ONE

AMERICA HAS A RETIREMENT PROBLEM

Retirement is not new. Americans have been retiring for centuries, but the main concern we have for our own retirement is much different now than what it was even a few years ago. If you were to go back to 2018, and you were in Las Vegas, Nevada at the Flamingo Hilton waiting with a bunch of retirees for the Donnie and Mary Osmond Concert to start and you asked them, "What is your biggest worry?" Most of them would have told you it was the fear of dying. With the uncertainty of the next life and the joy they were finding in this life, dying did not sound very appealing. Especially since so many of them were enjoying things like shopping, golfing, playing pickleball, spending time with the grandkids and traveling. Retirees wanted to stay on this earth as long as they could.

Unfortunately, things have changed over the last few years. Imagine you were to be in Memphis, Tennessee sitting on a tour bus with a bunch of retirees who had just finished walking down Beale Street and were on their way to Graceland and you asked them, "What is your biggest worry?" The answer you would hear from the majority of those on the bus would be vastly different than the one you heard back in Las Vegas in 2018.

Current statistics show 68% of retirees are now more concerned they will run out of money before they run out of retirement than they are about dying. This means that if you were to attend a funeral with a large group of retirees most of them would now rather be in the casket than in the pew. And what is even more troubling about this new statistic is it is not like most of life's worries where nothing comes of it. Current statistics show that over 50% of retirees will run out of money in retirement and die broke.

Many things contribute to the problem, but there are two main things you can attribute this failure to for most retirees. First, most people are not saving at the rates they should be saving for their retirement. A 35-year-old should have about one and a half times their salary saved. A 45-year-old should have up to four times their salary saved. A 55-year-old should have up to eight times their salary saved. And a 65-year-old should have up to 13.5 times their salary saved. Currently, about 1 in 4 Americans have nothing saved for their retirement, and over half of America has not saved at the levels they should have. Second, current retirees are subject to higher levels of financial risk during their retirement years than their parents and grandparents, and traditional retirement plans are not designed to address these risks.

A GLIMPSE INTO THE HISTORY OF RETIREMENT PLANNING IN THE U.S.

In the early 1930s many American retirees were faced with a financial crisis. Part of what led to the crisis had been brewing for decades but finally reached a tipping point in 1920. This was the first time in American history, where due to relocation, more people were living in cities than on farms. This meant a change from the extended family community (grandparents, parents, children, and cousins) to the nuclear family community (parents and children) we have today. It also meant a change in the financial stability of many retirees and the way they got cared for. Extended families were no longer able to take care of their aging family members because they were now living in separate cities. Then in 1929, the stock market crashed, taking with it the excess wealth and jobs of many retirees. By the early 1930s, over 50% of retirees found themselves unemployable and living below the poverty level for the first time in their lives with no workable solution to the problem anywhere in sight.

Finally, after months of research and studying what other countries were doing, the Social Security Act was drafted and signed into law by President Franklin D. Roosevelt on August 14, 1935. This began the process of getting many of the retirees who had been living below the poverty level into a sustainable lifestyle. Thanks to other wise leaders who came along during times the program was faltering like Ronald Reagan, Social Security has become the financial foundation for most retirees. Social Security currently provides monthly income benefits for 96% of retirees and these checks have transitioned America to where now less than 10% of her retirees live below the poverty level. But even as great as Social Security is, please don't expect Social Security to be your only source of income in retirement. If you do, you may find yourself above the poverty level, but with a lower standard of living than you had during your working years. Social Security was never designed to cover all your living costs during retirement.

People often ask, "If the program is so good, why don't 100% of retirees get Social Security?" For two reasons. First, some people have saved so much money they choose not to take the benefits they are entitled to in hopes of giving back to the program, since the money they receive from Social Security will not impact their lifestyle. Second, because there is a small percentage of the population that doesn't have enough work credits to qualify for Social Security benefits.

PENSIONS MAKE A COMEBACK

With Social Security firmly in place, Americans began looking for other solutions to secure their retirement future, so they once again turned to pensions starting in the 1940s. Alfred Dolge Company started the first pension back in 1882, but many of the early pensions failed, with Alfred Dolge's pension being the first one to go under. But with increased government regulation and time, new pensions had stabilized and by the early 1970s Social Security and pensions had become the one-two punch to secure the retirements for most Americans. Due to their functionality and their ability to help attract and retain workers, pensions became so popular that during the 1970s a large share of American workers had one, including my dad. If you know anything about railroad retirement benefits you know that the tier one benefits are

Social Security and tier two benefits are pension benefits. Had my dad not had these extra pension benefits, his retirement would have been worse than it already was.

THE 1970S CHANGED RETIREMENT PLANS FOREVER

In 1974, with the invention of the individual retirement account (IRA), everything started to change for the retirement plans of most Americans. Individuals now had their own option of saving for their retirement, but this transition would come at a high cost. The creation of the IRA opened the door for employers to start considering innovative ways of removing the financial burden pension plans were putting on the future finances of their companies and moving this liability onto the backs of their employees. The culmination of this opportunity presented itself in the late 70s, with the creation of the 401(k). Congress passed the Revenue Act of 1978 including a provision — Section 401(k) — that gave employees a tax-free way to defer compensation from bonuses or stock options. The law went into effect on January 1, 1980. This is when retirement for most Americans started the transition from a secure employer-based retirement of the past into the unsecure employee-based retirements we have today that I will refer to in this book as the traditional retirement plan.

THE TRADITIONAL RETIREMENT PLAN

Tax-Free

Taxable

Tax-Deferred

Social Security

The problem with this new change in retirement planning is the intent of the 401(k) was never to be a full replacement for pensions. Many early backers of the 401(k), including its founder Ted Benna, confirm they didn't design the 401(k) to be a primary retirement tool. Others say the popularity of 401(k) plans has exposed workers to big drops in the stock market and high fees from Wall Street money managers that many of these plans are struggling to overcome. Benna also acknowledged recently that he knew the 401(k) was going to be big, but he had no idea it would be the primary way people would accumulate money for retirement 30+ years later.

TAXES BECAME THE TAIL THAT WAGGED THE DOG BY THE 1980S

Even though people were not excited about losing their pension plans, they did get excited about the way these new IRA and 401(k) accounts were being treated for tax purposes. Not only were future retirees now able to contribute thousands of dollars into these plans without any current tax consequences, but they would also not have to pay taxes on the money in these accounts until years later. The tax on this money would not be due until it was pulled out in retirement. Which hopefully meant for those choosing to delay their taxes that they would be paying the taxes at a lower tax rate than what they would have paid up front. This turned into a sound strategy, especially for those who started deferring their taxes back in the 1970s. Our top marginal tax bracket today is 33% lower than the top marginal tax bracket during the 70s, which means a huge savings for those paying taxes today on money they deferred back then.

TRADITIONAL RETIREMENT PLANS BECAME COOKIE CUTTER BY THE 1990S

Traditional retirement plans became the standard because they are so simple to create and understand. They are put together using four basic variables. First, what average rate of return do you expect to get? Second, what average annual inflation rate do you expect over your lifetime? Third, how many years do you expect your retirement to last? Fourth, how much do you want to spend each year in retirement? If an advisor can get this basic information, he can use software to easily calculate how much money one will need to have when they retire along with a simple roadmap on how to get there.

For many of you, what I have explained about traditional retirement planning in this chapter sounds familiar because either you or a family member may still be using this type of planning for your own retirement. In fact, you may still feel very comfortable with your traditional retirement plan and how you think it will play out for your retirement. You may even be wondering why you should go through the hassle to change everything you spent so much time and money putting together. The reason you need to change from your traditional retirement plan is because your traditional retirement plan is not designed to address all the risks you will face during retirement, which means many of these plans will fail and yours may be one of them.

Traditional retirement plans are designed to get you to retirement and to give you some hope you can make it to the other side without running out of money, but they do little to provide you with what you need to get safely through retirement. To get safely through retirement, your plan will need to address the Top 10 Risks Facing Your Retirement and include strategies to reduce or eliminate each risk.

RISK-BASED RETIREMENT PLANNING IS BORN IN 2020

After decades of testing traditional retirement plans and realizing they were not going to provide the safety in retirement I was hoping for, I was finally able to put all the pieces together to create the risk-based retirement plan. This plan is designed to identify and eliminate the financial risks facing your retirement. Although the process took a lot of time and money for me to figure out, it can be very simple to apply to your own retirement. You will learn more about how I can help you later in the book, but it's now time to disclose the Top 10 Risks Facing Your Retirement.

THE TOP 10 FINANCIAL RISKS FACING YOUR RETIREMENT

1. SOCIAL SECURITY RISK

2. TAX RATE RISK

3. LONGEVITY RISK

4. SEQUENCE OF RETURN RISK

5. WITHDRAWAL RATE RISK

6. LONG-TERM CARE RISK

7. INFLATION RISK

8. MEDICARE RISK

9. ELDER ABUSE RISK

10. LACK OF INCOME DIVERSITY RISK

CHAPTER TWO

HAVE RETIREMENT PLANS ALWAYS BEEN SUBJECT TO ALL THESE RISKS?

The short answer, as well as the long answer, is no. Past generations did not face these same risks because retirement was different back then. People worked longer in comparison to their life expectancy than they do today. Often people not only worked past the average retirement age, which was age 65, but many of them worked up until the day they died. This resulted in a more consistent income stream during life's later years, which meant less risk and uncertainty.

RETIREES HAD PENSIONS

When you look back into the retirement plans of the 1970s, what you will find is at least 50% of retirees had pensions. This meant that most of America could secure their retirement by combining their Social Security and their pension to provide a guaranteed stream of income that would last as long as they did.

With Social Security and their pension plan covering the majority, if not all, of their living costs, retirees were able to use their retirement savings to cover unexpected expenses or aspirational goals. With so much guaranteed income many of the retirement risks we worry about today, such as longevity risk, withdrawal rate risk, and sequence of return risk, were irrelevant to these individuals.

Today only about 13% of retirees have pensions. This means we do not have the guaranteed income that was such a critical part of our predecessors' retirement. Because of this, many retirees are having to use the money they saved for basic living expenses, which leaves very little left to cover unexpected expenses or aspirational goals.

LIFE EXPECTANCY WAS SHORTER

Life expectancy back in 1970 was almost seven years less than it is today. The government estimated life expectancy in the 1970s to be about 70 years old. Today the government estimates life expectancy to be closer to 76.5. The shorter your life expectancy, the less you will need to worry about the risks facing your retirement.

THERE WAS LESS VOLATILITY AND UNCERTAINTY

For most people, either you had money or did not. If you had money, you could figure out with some certainty what your retirement would look like. Financial planners had basic software or fancy spreadsheets they would use to analyze your financial facts and circumstances to create a plan. This plan would include how much money you could spend per year in retirement to prevent running out of funds.

If you did not have money and were fully dependent on Social Security, you could also calculate with some certainty what retirement would look like. The problem here though is the results usually were not what people were hoping for because Social Security alone was not going to allow them to live the same lifestyle they once did.

Retirees today are faced with a very uncertain future. We are starting to see large swings in the market. There are innovative products that are disrupting traditional investment models like cryptocurrency and NFTs. And the government has more debt than we have ever had to deal with before, which means at some point there will be a day of reckoning that could cause taxes to double, leaving less money for your retirement. All of this leads to a retirement environment that is very uncertain and full of pitfalls.

IMPORTANT CONSIDERATIONS FOR EVERYONE

One of the first things you should know about your retirement is that it is going to look different from your parents, your friends at work, your neighbors, and it will definitely look different than those perfect retirements you see in online and television ads. And it is okay! Retirement was never meant to come off an assembly line like a Model-T Ford. Retirement was always meant to be different, so it could match with the variety of people who are ready to transition into this phase of life. But even with the differences we all have, there are foundational principles everyone must consider as we start planning for our retirement.

HEALTH IN RETIREMENT

This may be the single biggest factor you will need to consider for your retirement, because your health will impact your life expectancy, your medical costs in retirement and, the amount of money you will spend for daily living expenses. The longer you live, the more money you will need and the more financial risks you will face. If you are like my parents and pass away in your early 60s or 70s, the amount of money you will spend in retirement will be much less than what my wife's grandmother spent. She just passed away at the age of 97. Lucky for her, the medical costs were low because she did not spend even one day in the hospital after she retired, but she still needed far more money for her retirement than my parents did because her retirement lasted so long. My wife's grandmother was so healthy that up until 96 she was still climbing her apricot trees to pick the fruit. My father-in-law had to go out multiple times to try to get her off the latter and into the house, all the while reminding her that if she were to fall out of the tree and break her hip it would probably be the end of her.

It is estimated that the average male will spend $150,000 on medical costs during retirement and the average female will spend $135,000 on medical costs during retirement and these costs are going up. But remember, none of us are average (except for the family with 2.6 kids). So, depending on your health you may spend far more or far less than the average amount the government has told you to allocate for healthcare costs in retirement.

A good understanding of your health and life expectancy is important because it can impact various decisions you will need to make for your retirement. It can impact when you retire. If you are only expected to live until age 72, or are facing potential health issues, you may want to retire earlier than you would if you were going to be in good health and live into your 90s.

Your health can impact when you take your Social Security. If you are expected to live past age 90, taking Social Security at age 62 will not be the best financial decision for you. If you are married, your health can also impact whose life expectancy you should base your planning around. One of the tragedies I see as a retirement risk advisor is far too many married couples plan their retirement around the husband's life expectancy. This is problematic because the wife is often younger and expected to live longer. When this happens, the wife may be left to struggle through a much lower lifestyle during her remaining retirement years than she was enjoying prior to her husband's death. This lifestyle transition doesn't usually happen overnight, but the longer the surviving spouse lives the more financial issues she will have. If you are a married man reading this book and you make the financial decisions around your house, I ask you to do better than many of your peers. Make sure you are planning for both yours and your wife's retirement.

Here are some things each of us need to consider in relation to our health in retirement.

1. **Quality of retirement**—Health issues may inspire traveling and doing adventures early in retirement while you are still in good health. If this is the case, you will need more money in the early years and less money in the later years of your retirement.

2. **Medical costs**—Medicare will only cover so much of your medical expenses during your retirement years. If you have

medical conditions, you will require treatment during your retirement years and you will need more money set aside than those who are healthy. You will need funds available to cover medical premiums, deductibles, co-pays, and co-insurance. You can save this money through your normal investment accounts, or you can save your money in a health savings account (HSA) if you have access to one. An HSA offers tax-free benefits that your normal investment accounts do not.

3. **Longevity**—If I were to ask you to give me the age you expected to pass away, what I would find is that there is a higher probability that you will live longer than the age you give me. People are consistently underestimating how long they will live. Which means, people are outliving their retirement assets, because they did not expect to be around so long. Much like me that day in the desert with Todd. Had I realized I was going on over a six-mile round trip hike having to carry Todd much of the way, I would have planned differently. Longevity may also be longer than you anticipate due to ailments that cause you to feel unhealthy like a bad knee or a bad back, but are ailments that do not shorten your life expectancy. Which means you will need more money for retirement than anticipated to cover the living costs for these additional years.

WEALTH IN RETIREMENT

As I mentioned at the start of this book, I was raised in a home where we barely had enough money to survive. Our finances always seemed to work out, but this experience provided me with an important realization. The amount of money you have available to spend and invest has a significant impact on your freedom and the decisions you can make to secure your future. I remember my family running out of money multiple times before we ran out of month. This meant that we were unable to do anything that cost money, including shopping for groceries many times, until my dad's check showed up in the mail. I also remember occasionally being able to go to the movies or other activities because my parents felt they had a few extra dollars at the time.

As you look to your retirement, it is important to consider how much money you will need. Are you one who is happy to live a simpler life in retirement, or have you been waiting for retirement so you can travel the world? Either of these options may be the right one for you, but you need to know what your plan is so you can save the money you will need to cover your expected lifestyle in retirement. There are two questions you must ask yourself about your money if you are serious about creating a retirement plan to fit your goals and ambitions. Both questions will go a long way in helping you to plan out your retirement. The first question is, what do you want your money to do while you are alive? Do you want to live as a minimalist trying to see how little money you can spend; do you want to live a lifestyle that is way above what you were able to live during your working years; or do you want a retirement that is somewhere in between these two? The second question is, what do you want your money to do once you die? Are you okay to bounce the check to the mortuary upon your death or do you want to leave a legacy others can remember you for? There is no right or wrong answer to either of these questions, but they both must be answered if you want any hope of reaching your goals using your retirement plan.

As we have switched from the employer-funded retirement plans of the 1970s to the traditional retirement plans of today, wealth available for retirement has become a much larger factor in determining your retirement lifestyle. The amount of wealth you have will also provide insight into how much planning you will need to do for your retirement. I talk to thousands of people about retirement on an annual basis, and I have come across a small segment of the population that no matter how little planning they do, they will not run out of money in retirement. For most of these individuals, it is because they have lived a life where they have made far more money than they spent. Yet, what I find with most people I talk to is that they have not saved enough money for their retirement. This means figuring out what money will be available at retirement becomes a critical part of determining retirement lifestyle.

Here are a few things to consider:

1. **Assets available**—The government tells us the average American should have right around $375,000 set aside for their retirement, but the average retiree only has about $50,000 saved. You need to start figuring out if you will have the assets you need to fund your retirement, or if you will need to adjust your plan. If you are an above average income earner, you may need much more than the government average to cover your expected retirement lifestyle.

2. **Income needs**—Do you want to maintain your pre-retirement lifestyle? If you do, it is going to require 70 to 80% of your pre-retirement income, especially during the initial

years of retirement. The old paradigm of retirement planning showed that most retirees could live off about 50% of their pre-retirement income, but today's statistics show many Americans will need much more income than this due to increased costs and longevity.

3. **Social Security**— People are often under the misconception that Social Security should provide them with the same lifestyle in retirement as they were living pre-retirement. In fact, some of you may have seen the popular question going around social media during the pandemic that said something like this, "Why are we paying the unemployed so much, when we expect Social Security recipients to live off of so little?" The person who posted this question must not have understood that Social Security was never intended to provide all the income a retiree would need to live off during retirement. Social Security was designed to only provide about 40% of retirement income for the average retiree.

An important question you need to answer for yourself as you plan for your own retirement is, "How much after-tax income will it take to maintain the lifestyle I want in retirement, and what do I need to do to have that much income available?

RISKS IN RETIREMENT

If you are like most Americans, you have spent your working years doing everything you can to protect yourself from the daily risks of life. If you own a home, chances are you have purchased homeowner's insurance to protect your home in case of a fire or a flood. If you own a car, you have purchased car insurance to protect you in case you get into an accident and total your car. Yet, in retirement very few people are doing anything to protect themselves against the financial risks brought about by being permanently unemployed for a period of 20, 30, even 40 years.

The main reason this happens is because people are unaware that many of these financial risks even exist. These risks are not explained by teachers in school or even by most financial advisors. I wish they were, but they are not, which means many of you have a problem. Because lack of awareness may be a good excuse when trying to talk yourself out of a ticket or trying to explain why you missed a family event, but it does nothing to eliminate the risks facing your retirement.

You need to do a better job of preparing yourself and your loved ones for the financial risks you will face in retirement, and here are some things you should consider.

1. **Identify the risks** – It is hard to eliminate the financial risks facing your retirement if you do not know what they are and what effect they can have on your retirement. Therefore, you must identify the financial risks facing your retirement and learn what effects each risk can have on you and your loved ones. I will be covering the Top 10 Financial Risks Facing Your Retirement in this book but know there may be other risks you will encounter along the way that this book does not cover.

2. **Risk tolerance** – Can your emotions handle a 40% drop in the stock market? Can you make up the financial shortfall if taxes double? Can you fund a long-term care event with

the money you have saved? Can you be okay if you run out of money in retirement? Only you can answer these questions, but they must be answered. If your risk tolerance is such you can be okay with any, or all, of these risks then your retirement plan will look different from someone who wants to remove these risks from their retirement.

3. **Eliminating risk** – In most cases the financial risks facing your retirement are not going to just disappear. You are going to have to take some form of action to eliminate these risks from your retirement. You must determine for yourself what steps you are willing to take to eliminate the various financial risks you may face in the future.

It is now time to go through The Top 10 Risks Facing Your Retirement I introduced in Chapter 1. Please know there is no preset order to how you should educate yourself on each of these risks, so you can skip around the chapters on each of these risks if you choose. The critical part, if you want a safe and secure retirement, is to know what each risk is and to understand the impact it will have on your retirement. You then have a choice. You can either choose to accept some or maybe even all of the risks facing your retirement or you can put in the effort it will take to reduce or eliminate each risk from your retirement.

CHAPTER THREE

RISK #1: SOCIAL SECURITY RISK

Social Security risk consists of two risks. The first is the risk of claiming your benefits at the wrong time. And the second is the risk that you will have to pay taxes on your Social Security benefits.

People have a lot of misconceptions about Social Security and these misconceptions are leading to financial issues for many retirees. Someone who is entitled to $1,000 in Social Security benefits at a full retirement age 67 could end up losing as much as $540 a month in benefits if they claim at 62 versus those who wait until 70. Think of those family members or friends you know who are in their late 80s or early 90s. How much of a difference would $540 a month of additional income make in their retirement? This additional money could buy a lot of groceries, help pay for utilities, or provide a cushion from other monthly expenses.

Advertising agencies and the government are both to blame for the problem. Advertising agencies have drilled instant gratification into your brain for decades. Which means you have been trained to believe that once something becomes available, including your Social Security benefits, there is no need to wait - you should take advantage of it immediately. The government has led you to believe that it does not matter when you claim your Social Security benefits, it is six of one and half-dozen of another. Based upon their life expectancy calculation the government projects breakeven will occur after most people have passed away no matter when they claim their Social Security benefits, so why wait? The problem is the life expectancy tables the government uses are incorrect once you reach retirement age.

As a result of both ad agencies and the government, far too many retirees are claiming their Social Security benefits at age 62 when they first become available. By doing this, many of these retirees are missing out on tens of thousands of dollars they could have received had they been willing to wait until they got older.

1- RISK OF CLAIMING SOCIAL SECURITY BENEFITS AT THE WRONG TIME

As just mentioned, the government would like you to believe that it does not matter when you claim your Social Security benefits (62, full retirement age, 70, or anywhere in between), because by the time you pass away it will be six of one and half-dozen of another. But reality is not always what the government would like you to believe it is.

When the government does their calculation for Social Security breakeven, they include infant mortality, accidents that happen during your working years, drug overdoses, and any other premature death. Using these assumptions, the government estimates current life expectancy to be right around 76.5 years old. If life expectancy is only 76.5, then Social Security breakeven for almost every scenario will not happen until after most of you are expected to have passed away. Therefore, the age you claim your Social Security benefits really does not matter. If you make it to retirement, you have crossed several hurdles that would have reduced your life expectancy, which means your new life expectancy is no longer 76.5. It has increased substantially. If you make it to age 65, your average life expectancy if you are a male has increased to around age 84, and if you are a female it has increased to around age 88.

When you take these higher life expectancies into consideration, you will find that the results for Social Security breakeven are just the opposite of what the government has promoted. Under almost every scenario breakeven for Social Security is now going to happen before average life expectancy. This means if you claim your benefits too early you could leave tens, if not hundreds of thousands of dollars on the table. Later in this section I will cover how you can calculate the right age for you to start taking your Social Security benefits.

I would also caution those of you who think you can beat the system by taking your Social Security benefits at age 62 and investing the money you receive each year until you reach age 70. By investing what you have saved and matching it with your Social Security payment, the hope is to have a much higher monthly payment than if you had just waited until age 70 to claim your benefits. I have found that there are two problems with this strategy. First, most of you will never end up investing the money. You think you will, but when it comes down to it the money gets spent.

Second, unless you can guarantee high rates of return over decades of investing, the internal increases offered by Social Security for waiting until age 70 will beat your portfolio in the long run. Not only are delayed retirement credits available for waiting until age 70, but Social Security also provides an annual cost of living adjustment (COLA) to your Social Security benefits for the rest of your life.

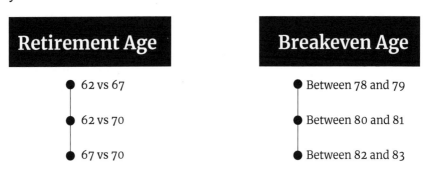

Retirement Age	Breakeven Age
● 62 vs 67	● Between 78 and 79
● 62 vs 70	● Between 80 and 81
● 67 vs 70	● Between 82 and 83

WHAT IS MY FULL RETIREMENT AGE?

In the late 1970s, Social Security was starting to experience some major financial issues. In response to these issues, President Ronald Reagan was finally able to bring both sides of the aisle together to pass the Social Security Amendment of 1983 to fix the program. Part of this legislation included increasing the full retirement age for most Americans. The following chart will help you understand what your full retirement age is.

Born 1943 - 1954 – 66 years old	1955 - 66 years 2 months
	1956 - 66 years 4 months
	1957 - 66 years 6 months
Born 1960 or later – Month you turn age 67	1958 - 66 years 8 months
	1959 - 66 years 10 months

WHY IS MY FULL RETIREMENT AGE IMPORTANT?

The benefits you are entitled to from Social Security are based upon your full retirement age. At your full retirement age, you are entitled to 100% of your Social Security benefits. If you decide to take your benefits earlier than your full retirement age, there will be consequences. If you decide to wait until after your full retirement age to take your Social Security, there will be benefits.

If you claim your Social Security prior to your full retirement age, your benefit will be reduced by five-ninths of one percent for each month before full retirement age up to 36 months. If the number of months exceeds 36, then the benefit is further reduced by five-twelve of one percent per month.

Example: Armando will turn 62 soon and wants to start claiming his Social Security benefits. At his full retirement age of 67, he is eligible for $1,000 in monthly benefits. If Armando goes ahead with his plan, he will only receive $700 in monthly benefits.

If you wait to claim your Social Security benefits until after your full retirement age, up until age 70, you will be entitled to delayed retirement credits. Because of these credits, your Social Security benefits will be increased by two-thirds of one percent per month. This adds up to 8% for each full year you wait.

Example: Maria's full retirement age is 67 years old. At this age, she is entitled to $1,000 in monthly Social Security benefits. If she decides to wait until age 70 to claim her benefits, she will be entitled to a monthly benefit of $1,240.

As you can see from the two examples, there is a significant difference in the Social Security benefits you will receive based on when you file for benefits, and these benefits are permanent. If you start claiming your benefits at 62, this is the benefit you will receive for the rest of your life, and maybe even your spouse's life after you die—so choose wisely. There are three ways to reverse your decision if you have claimed your Social Security benefits and have changed your mind, but very few people ever do any of them.

Do Over – If you are younger than full retirement age when you apply for benefits, you will have 12 months from the time you applied for Social Security to request a "do over" if you change your mind. This will require you to complete form SSA – 521 and pay back all benefits you have received. If you had any family members who started taking benefits off your work record during this time, they must consent in writing to the "do over," and all the money they have received from Social Security must be paid back as well.

Go Back to Work – If your income exceeds certain thresholds prior to full retirement age, any Social Security benefits you are receiving will be reduced or eliminated. Any benefits you lose because you went back to work will be added back into the future benefits you will receive once you apply for benefits again.

2023 SOCIAL SECURITY EARNINGS LIMITS

Under full retirement age	Year you reach full retirement age	At full retirement month
• Limit - $21,240/Year ($1,770/Month)	• Limit - $56,520/Year ($4,710/Month)	• Work as much as you want
• $1 for each $2 over threshold	• $1 for each $3 over threshold	

*Earnings only include income subject to Social Security taxation.

Suspend Benefits after Full Retirement Age – Once you have reached full retirement age you can suspend your Social Security benefits at any time, up until age 70. Any benefits you suspend during this period will be added to your Social Security account, so you will get a higher monthly payment in the future.

SOCIAL SECURITY PLANNING IS A FAMILY AFFAIR

In addition to providing you with benefits based upon your work record, Social Security also offers benefits to your qualifying family members. If you are married or have other qualifying family members their benefits need to be taken into consideration when determining the best claiming strategy. Here is a list of people who may qualify to receive Social Security benefits on your work record and whom you should consider into any claiming strategy.

- Spouse
- Children
- Former Spouse
- Parents*
- Grandchildren**

*Parents are only eligible for survivor benefits, and they must have been your dependent at the time of your death.

**There are strict rules for grandchildren to qualify for any benefits.

WHEN SHOULD I CLAIM MY SOCIAL SECURITY TO MAXIMIZE MY BENEFITS?

If you are single or the higher income earner in your marriage and you expect to live to life expectancy, you will get the maximum benefit by waiting until age 70 to file for Social Security. If you do not have a work record and are going to claim on your spouse's work record for your benefit, waiting until your full retirement age will provide the greatest benefit. If you are the lower earning spouse, or you do not think you or your spouse will live to life expectancy, you will need to use a Social Security benefits calculator to figure out the best age for you to claim your benefits. There are many third-party software providers who can help you do the calculation, or you can go to www.ssa.gov and use the calculator provided by the government. Be careful when it comes to estimating your life expectancy. Remember, many of you will live much longer than you think you will.

2 - RISK OF PAYING TAXES ON MY SOCIAL SECURITY BENEFITS

When taxes were first imposed on Social Security back in 1983 there were only about 10% of retirees who had to pay tax on their benefits. Currently, over 40% of retirees are paying taxes on their Social Security benefits. Over the next decade the number of retirees who will pay tax on their benefits will continue to go up due to COLA adjustments and fixed provisional income thresholds. The problem is if you happen to be one of these retirees you could run out of money 5 to 7 years faster than you otherwise would.

WHAT IS PROVISIONAL INCOME?

This is the combined income which the government uses to determine if the IRS will tax your Social Security benefits or not.

WHAT IS INCLUDED IN PROVISIONAL INCOME?

Provisional income includes all earned income, distributions from qualified plans, required minimum distributions (RMDs), 1099s from taxable accounts, pensions, rental income, interest from municipal bonds, and one-half of your Social Security. A simpler way to say this is take all taxable income, your tax-exempt interest income, and one half of your Social Security and this is your provisional income.

A closer look at the types of income included in the provisional income calculation reveals that there are two types of retirement income you do not need to include in your calculation. The first one is any type of income with Roth in the title – Roth IRA, Roth 401(k), or Roth annuity. The other one is distributions from permanent life insurance policies if you have met the tax-free guidelines of the policy.

WHAT ARE THE PROVISIONAL INCOME THRESHOLDS?

The Social Security Administration established thresholds so that the lowest income earners would not have to pay tax on their Social Security, and the highest earners would pay tax on up to 85% of their Social Security benefits. The thresholds are the same as they were in 1993. This is something most retirees still complain about but there is no plan in place to increase the provisional income thresholds. The reason is because the taxes paid by the retirees who are subject to this tax have become an important part of the income Social Security receives each year. I wish I had better news for the future, but it does not appear there will be any changes to these thresholds anytime soon.

Married Filing Joint

Provisional Income	Percent of Social Security Subject to Tax
Under $32,000	0%
$32,000 to $44,000	Up to 50%
Above $44,000	Up to 85%

Single

Provisional Income	Percent of Social Security Subject to Tax
Under $25,000	0%
$25,000 to $34,000	Up to 50%
Above $34,000	Up to 85%

WHAT IS THE PROBLEM WITH PAYING TAX ON MY SOCIAL SECURITY?

If you end up having to pay tax on your Social Security benefits you will have less money to live off in retirement. The taxes you pay on your Social Security benefits will require you to draw down your retirement assets at a faster pace. But this may just be the beginning of your problems because the income needed to pay this tax is often taken from tax-deferred accounts. If this happens, you will also owe tax on the additional money you pull out from the tax-deferred account, which will mean you have even less money for your retirement.

Social Security is inflation-adjusted each year. This means you will get more income from Social Security each year, which is a good thing, but you will also have to pay more tax each year.

Then there is the opportunity cost. There is a high probability you will make more money from your investments in retirement than you did during your working years. But if this money is no longer available to invest because you used the money to pay taxes, the opportunity for growth on this money is lost.

It is estimated that the average person who pays tax on their Social Security benefits will run out of retirement assets 5 to 7 years faster than those who do not. In an environment where life expectancy is on a steady increase, the last thing you want to have happen to your retirement assets is for them to run out faster than expected.

Many people are under the misconception that there is an age to which you will no longer be subject to the provisional income rules. This is not true, but after having been asked the question so many times, I think I have finally figured out where the misconception started. It started with the retired guys who go to the local deli to solve the world's problems. Eventually, the topic of conversation gets to retirement and the younger guys start complaining to the older guys about the tax they pay on their Social Security. Then one of the older guys decides it is time to share his wisdom, so he lets the younger guys know he no longer pays tax on his Social Security benefits. Realizing what a reaction this new piece of wisdom created amongst the younger guys, two or three more of the older wise guys confirm they no longer pay taxes on their Social Security benefits either.

The problem is these older wisemen are like the gambler who only talks about his winning and never his losses, as these men have failed to include an important part of the story. What they failed to include is the fact that it was not because the laws changed as they got older. It is because they ran out of money in their IRA and 401(k) so they no longer have enough provisional income for their Social Security to be taxed.

HOW DID THE GOVERNMENT PICK 85% AS THE TAXABLE PORTION?

Your Social Security benefits are made up of three different pools of money – your contributions, employer contributions, and growth on these contributions. The government estimates only 15% of the Social Security benefits you receive are from what you contributed into your account during your working years from money you paid taxes on; therefore, the other 85% is subject to tax.

HOW DO I KEEP FROM PAYING TAXES ON MY SOCIAL SECURITY BENEFITS?

You need to make sure your provisional income is not higher than the provisional income threshold. There are two ways to do this, but I do not recommend the first option. First, you can make sure you do not have enough income in retirement to exceed the provisional income threshold. The problem with this option is that there is a high probability you will have a less than stellar retirement. Second, is to not have enough taxable income in retirement to exceed the provisional income thresholds. You can do this by transitioning most of your retirement assets into Roth accounts and permanent life insurance products. You will then use the income from these accounts as your main source of income during your retirement years. As mentioned earlier in this book, income from Roth accounts and permanent life insurance products is not subject to the provisional income calculation, which means you get a double win. A better lifestyle in retirement and no tax on your Social Security benefits.

There are some who worry that the laws will change in the future on how the government handles the tax on Roth accounts and permanent life insurance as it relates to Social Security, but as of the writing of this book nothing has been proposed. I will explain later in this book how you need to structure your retirement to get your Social Security income tax-free.

To get access to your Social Security statement go to www. ssa.gov and sign up for an account.

PRO TIP

Use your Social Security statement to keep up on the benefits you and your family are eligible for so you can include these amounts in your retirement planning.

CHAPTER FOUR

RISK #2:
TAX RATE RISK

Tax rate risk is the risk taxes will be higher in the future than they are today.

In the 1970s, when tax-deferred accounts were established, tax rates were as high as 70%. Nobody could imagine they could ever go higher, so tax-deferred investing became the investment of choice. Fast forward fifty years, and we find that those who invested in tax-deferred accounts were right. Especially since the highest marginal tax rate today is less than 40%. But we are not living in the 70s, although when I look at some of the current clothing trends I sometimes beg to differ. Today we have some of the lowest tax rates we have ever seen in the history of America. There have only been four other times since taxes were brought about in 1913 that taxes have been lower than they are today, but can they stay this way? Not if we expect the U.S. government to continue paying their debts and obligations. The government has three main financial obligations they are responsible for that could cause tax rates to be higher in the future, maybe even double what they are today. They are Social Security, Medicare, and the national debt.

"REGARDLESS OF WHAT POLITICIANS TELL YOU, ANY ADDITIONAL ACCUMULATIONS OF DEBT ARE, ABSENT DRAMATIC REDUCTIONS IN THE SIZE AND ROLE OF GOVERNMENT, BASICALLY DEFERRED TAX INCREASES...UNLESS WE BEGIN TO GET OUR FISCAL HOUSE IN ORDER, THERE'S SIMPLY NO OTHER WAY TO HANDLE OUR EVER-MOUNTING DEBT BURDENS EXCEPT BY DOUBLING TAXES OVER TIME."

– DAVID WALKER, FORMER COMPTROLLER GENERAL OF THE UNITED STATES

Social Security— For decades many people have been talking about how Social Security is underfunded and how you should not plan on it for your retirement. In fact, one of the top questions people have when I teach about Social Security is, "Is Social Security going broke?" And my answer is always the same, "Yes, Social Security is going broke, but it will never go broke." There are three main reasons for this. First, Social Security is the most popular entitlement program the government has, so it will get the votes needed to stabilize the program before it runs out of money. Second, there are several strategies available to fix the program. These include options like increasing the full retirement age, getting rid of deferred retirement credits, not letting people access their benefits until age 64, and increasing taxes. I do not suggest they do the following, but the government could fix Social Security indefinitely if they would raise the current Social Security payroll tax rate by 4.2%. This would mean a tax increase on Social Security taxed wages of 2.1% on the employer and 2.1% on the employee. I believe what will fix Social Security is a combination of changes as happened back in 1983. Third, if Social Security were to fail, the American economy would equally fail. There are over 40% of retirees who use Social Security as their only source of income, and 96% of retirees are receiving benefits from the program. If all these people lost the monthly income Social Security provides, the rest of the economy would not be able to sustain the financial shortfall that an event like this would create. All of this being said, you should know when changes happen to the Social Security program, which they will, they will not be implemented overnight. Current retirees will see very little, if any, changes to their current benefits.

If you look at the financial statements of the Social Security Trust Fund, you will find net equity of just under three trillion dollars. The net equity of the program shows its value if all its debts and liabilities are paid down and the health of the program itself. These financial statements make Social Security look like one of the most well-funded programs the government has, which, if you do not take into consideration future obligations the program owes, it currently is. But beginning in 2021, everything started to change. In 2021, Social Security started operating in the red for the first time since Ronald Reagan fixed the program back in 1983. Social Security will continue to lose money each year, and the trust fund will continue to be depleted until around 2035, at which point all the reserves will be gone. There will still be enough income for beneficiaries of the program to get between 75-80% of their current monthly income, but that is it.

What created the problem? The problem began right after World War II. The soldiers came home from war and started procreating at levels that had never been seen in the history of America. As a result of their procreation activities, this generation ended up with about 78,000,000 children. We call these children "baby boomers." But there was a significant difference between the baby boomers and their parents. These baby boomers did not have as much passion for children as their parents did. As a result, they ended up having 32,000,000 fewer children than their parents, and this created a demographic glitch.

We are now starting to see the effect of this glitch. First, as these baby boomers retire, it is leaving fewer people in the workforce. When Social Security first started, there were about 42 people working for every one person receiving benefits. Today there are only about 2.8 people working for every one person receiving benefits. And over the next decade, there will only be about two people working for every one person receiving benefits. Second, there are about 10,000 people signing up for Social Security each year, and there are only about 6,000 people leaving the program. This increase is going to continue for about another decade.

Medicare – Medicare is divided into four parts – Part A, Part B, Part C, and Part D. Medicare Part A and B are original, or traditional, Medicare. Medicare Parts C & D are add-ons to Medicare, and the benefits they offer are provided by third-party companies. Part C is Medicare Advantage Plans, and Part D is prescription drug coverage. Due to the structure of Medicare, the only part of Medicare having financial issues is Part A because it is the only part of Medicare with a trust fund and true accounting. Part A is the part of Medicare covering hospitalization and is the part of Medicare most of you will receive for free. This part of Medicare is currently scheduled to run out of money around 2028. But do not let smooth government accounting trick you into believing the rest of Medicare is on solid financial ground. Part B, the part of Medicare that covers general medical expenses you would have outside of a hospital and that you pay a portion of through monthly premiums, will start creating a drag on the general fund of the government within the decade. Parts C & D will only be stabilized through higher premiums you will pay to third-party companies.

The financial impact Medicare will have on the government will increase at a faster pace than even Social Security. The reason is that, in addition to having the same baby boomers signing up for Social Security as are signing up for Medicare, the cost of medical goods and services are going up at a rate higher than inflation. Over the last two decades alone medical costs have gone up almost 300%.

National debt—Our current national debt is out of control, and it does not take a rocket scientist to realize it is not going down anytime soon. As of January 2023, the national debt was over $31,000,000,000,000 (yes, folks, that is 12 zeros). Some of the country's top economists estimate the debt will balloon to around 50 trillion dollars sometime between 2028 and 2030. When the national debt gets to this level, what we will have is a situation where annual revenues of the government may only be enough to cover the interest on the national debt, leaving nothing to cover the costs associated with running the government and its various entitlement programs. This will leave us with no other option but to increase taxes.

Any one of these three liabilities by itself could cause taxes to rise, but when you put them all together within the same decade, what you find is a perfect storm for future tax rates to be much higher than they are today. We know taxes will go up for the first time on January 1, 2026, when the 2017 Tax Cuts and Jobs Act expires, but it is really 2030 I am worried about. This is when the culmination of liabilities owed for Social Security, Medicare, and the national debt will be at the highest level.

WHAT IS THE SOLUTION?

Tax-free investing. You want investments that will provide income streams free of federal tax, state tax, and capital gains tax and will not cause Social Security to be taxed. I will talk about what these investments are later in the book, but these types of investments include anything with Roth in the name and most permanent life insurance policies.

LOST DEDUCTIONS COULD INCREASE YOUR TAXABLE INCOME IN RETIREMENT

Brooke retired three years ago with an expectation that her taxes would be lower in retirement than they were during her working years, but this is not her reality. Frustrated with the situation, she decided to reach out to a local financial expert to see if she could give her some tips on what she could do.

After waiting on hold for a few minutes, Brooke was finally connected to the advisor. After going through basic pleasantries, the advisor asked, "Brooke, what can I help you with?" After providing a little of her backstory, Brooke shared her concern with the amount of taxes she was paying and said, "I do not get it. Why am I paying so many taxes in retirement? I did not think it was supposed to work this way". The advisor thanked Brooke for her question and then said, "Before I answer your question, I have a question for you. What can you tell me about your deductions?" Brooke laughed and giggled for what seemed like a minute before she responded, "What do you mean tell you about my deductions? I do not have any deductions. I lost those years ago." To which the advisor responded, "I think I see your problem."

In retirement, most of you are going to have a decrease in your gross income, but because of lost deductions you may find you do not have less taxable income. Here are a few of the big deductions many of you had available during your working years but may lose during your retirement years.

Mortgage interest – Many of you lost your mortgage interest deduction at the end of 2017 when the government signed the 2017 Tax Cuts and Jobs Act into law. The reason is because this new law increased the standard deduction to help simplify tax filing for most people. Now only about 10 to 15% of Americans itemize their deductions. But even if you did not get phased out of your mortgage deduction at the end of 2017, by the time you get to retirement your mortgage balance often is so low the interest you pay is providing little to no value on your taxes. Plus, we have recently experienced a period of historically low interest rates, which means even if you have a large mortgage, the interest you are paying may not be enough to provide much of a deduction.

Charitable contributions – As with everything else in our lives, there have been several surveys conducted on the charitable habits of those in retirement. These surveys revealed that if you were charitable during your working years, there is a high probability you will continue to be charitable during your retirement years. This is probably not a surprise to anyone, but what may be a surprise is how retirees approach their charitable contributions during retirement versus how they approached them during their working years. During the working years, what the surveys discovered is that people had more money but less time. As a result, their favorite method of giving was by donating money. They would write a check to their local food bank, church, or other charitable organization. But once people got into retirement, most of them had more time and less money, which meant instead of writing the check to the food bank, they would take a day out of their week and volunteer. Instead of paying for a child to go to summer camp for a week, they went themselves and donated their time as a camp counselor. To the organizations receiving the donation, the form the donation came in (money or service) really did not matter. Most organizations are very appreciative of whatever they can get, but to the IRS, it makes all the difference in the world. The IRS offers a deduction for donated money, but no such deduction exists for donated time.

Children – As a father of eight children, I have learned a lot about kids over the last three decades, including the tax benefits they can provide. There are two main benefits available for those of you with kids. The first is the child tax credit. This is a tax credit you receive for qualifying children living in your home who are under the age of 17. The second is the education credits you can get for paying for your kids' college. Both credits can result in you paying thousands of dollars less on your tax bill during your working years but will probably be gone once you get into retirement.

Not too long ago, I was having dinner with a friend and his wife at Vintner Grill on West Charleston in Summerlin, Nevada. As the evening proceeded, we got onto the topic of families, and I asked my friend about his two sons. He started off by talking about his older son, Barrett, who was living in Santa Barbara, California, at the time and how he had recently gotten a job at the local library. Then the conversation moved to his younger son, Spencer. My friend went on to explain how Spencer was a successful photographer but was back living with my friend and his wife while he worked on various online projects he had started. As my friend finished telling me about Spencer, his wife (who was not the mother of the two boys) said to my friend as she hit him on the shoulder, "We need to get Spencer out of the house. He is

40 years old." To which my friend responded back, "Oh sweetie, he's only 38." I do not care if your child is 38. I do not care if your child is 40, and I do not even care if they are still living in your home. But if they are still living in your home once they become adults, you are not getting any type of deduction from the IRS for them to help reduce your taxes.

Tax-deferred contributions – This is where I see the biggest problem for most of you. For most of you, your late 50s and early 60s is the time you will contribute the most amount of money to your tax-deferred retirement accounts. By this point, if you have kids, they are raised, and there is finally extra money to save for retirement. Under current laws, many retirees can contribute tens of thousands of dollars to these accounts during the years just prior to retirement.

But the game changes when you get into retirement. You do not want to keep contributing money into these accounts each year, you want to start taking distributions out so you can enjoy the fruits of your labor. This change from contributing to your retirement accounts to distributing from your retirement accounts means that you may have just lost one of the greatest benefits you had going for you to keep your taxes down.

PRO TIP

Take advantage of these historically low tax rates by doing some Roth conversions before taxes go back up.

CHAPTER FIVE

RISK #3: LONGEVITY RISK

Longevity risk is the risk you will outlive your retirement assets.

With life expectancy continuing to increase each year, the consequences longevity brings have become the biggest fear of many retirees. As mentioned earlier, if you make it to age 65, your average life expectancy as a male is around age 84 and as a female is around age 88. Over 25% of you will live past 90, and over 10% will live into your 100s. You may be surprised to find that some of you will spend as many years retired as you spent working.

As with many of the other risks covered in this book, the problem with longevity risk started with the creation of the IRA and 401(k). Since this time, many of you have struggled to save enough money to provide for a short life expectancy let alone one that is increasing each year. Which means many of you will be spending the last of your golden years trying to make ends meet using Social Security alone, which will leave you in need and wanting.

YOU WILL PROBABLY UNDERESTIMATE YOUR LIFE EXPECTANCY

Another problem with longevity is people are struggling to figure out how long they will live. If I were to ask you, and everyone else who reads this book, to provide me with the age that you believed you will live to, and then I were to follow the national obituaries looking for when each of you died (do not worry, I will not do this), statistics tell me I would discover an interesting problem. Over 50% of you would underestimate your life expectancy, and over 28% of you would underestimate it by at least five years. Retirees are running out of money left and right, and this error in calculating life expectancy is just adding to the problem.

LONGEVITY IS A RISK MULTIPLIER

Have you noticed the longer you own something, the more problems you start to have with the item? If you have bought a new car lately, you probably are not overly concerned the car is going to break down and leave you stranded, but even if it did the car would have some type of warranty to cover the costs. What if you have owned your car for 15 years? Your transmission is probably leaving fluid behind every time you stop, the new car smell has been replaced with the aroma of french fries, and the engine is sounding more like a jet every day.

If you have bought a new house lately you probably have not had many problems with it either, but even if you do, most new homes come with a one-year warranty. What if you have owned the house for 20 years? The roof has probably started to leak, the foundation is cracking and if you have as many kids as I do, you are on your third set of carpets.

Longevity creates this same issue for your retirement. The longer you live, the higher probability the risks I talk about in this book are going to start wreaking havoc on your retirement. And the real kicker is that life expectancy is going up, not down. Even the government is expecting average life expectancy to be between 85 and 86 by 2060. This means if you make it to retirement age in 2060 your true average life expectancy will be over age 90.

PRO TIP

Plan your retirement to last until age 100. You may not make it that long, but if you do, you will thank me later.

CHAPTER SIX

RISK #4: SEQUENCE OF RETURN RISK

Sequence of return risk is the risk that the market will be down during a time when you need to take distributions out of your retirement.

Most of you have lived through some type of market downturn during your working years, and you have lived to talk about it. In fact, if you held firm to a wise investment strategy after any major downturn in the market during your lifetime, your assets are worth more now than they were before the market dropped. This is because over time markets rebound and grow. But once you start approaching retirement, the ballgame starts to change. If the market drops and stays down for any length of time during the first 5-10 years of your retirement, your well-planned retirement can turn into a disaster rather quickly. This is because once you get into retirement you start taking distributions out of your investment accounts, which means you are locking in the investment losses for good. The assets you distribute will never have a chance to rebound. When this happens, your retirement assets can be reduced to half their original value in just a few years, as shown in this chart.

Year	Beginning-of-Year Average Account Value	Annual Return	End-of-Year Distribution	Account Value
1	$1,500,000	-9.00%	$67,500	$1,297,500
2	$1,297,500	-11.89%	$69,525	$1,073,702
3	$1,073,702	-22.10%	$71,610	$ 764,803

Withdrawal Rate in Year 1 = 4.5%
Withdrawal Rate in Year 2 =9.6%

And as you can see from the chart, retirement will look much different for you going forward if there is a substantial market loss during the early years of your retirement. Not only will you lose substantial assets, but after the market loss you may be forced into a higher withdrawal rate from your assets than is sustainable to support your desired lifestyle. A good solution to sequence of return risk is to include principal protected products as part of your retirement plan.

PRINCIPAL PROTECTED PRODUCTS

One of the best ways you can structure your retirement to eliminate risk is to include principal protected product as part of your investment mix. You need to protect the assets you cannot afford to lose. A good guideline for this is to protect your assets up to your age as a percentage of 100 just prior to retirement, or the bond portion of your portfolio during your working years.

Example: Kylee is age 60, and she expects to retire in five years. She wants to make sure once she gets into retirement, she is not subject to sequence of return risk. How much of her investment portfolio should Kylee have in principal protected products? Kylee should have 60%. The rest of her portfolio can be invested in higher risk assets to help increase her long-term rate of return.

Example: Cynetria has 20 years before she retires and is not happy with her 60% stock, 40% bond portfolio. She has been looking into principal protected products. How much of her portfolio should she move to principal protected? Cynetria should move 40%. All the money moved should come from the bond portion of her portfolio.

Here is a list of requirements a product must have to be deemed principal protected:

Guaranteed to Never Go Backward – This is the foundation of a principal protected product. You want to make sure that no matter what happens in the market your principal will be protected against loss.

Moderately Liquid – Principal protected products do not need to be fully liquid, but they do need to be structured to where you can get a portion of the money out each year if you need it. Remember one of the purposes of principal protection is to protect you if there is a down market. Since you do not know when this will happen it is important you have an investment you can get access to immediately if the markets turn.

Backed by the Government – With government backing comes more protection. Therefore, you want principal protected products that offer some type of guarantee from either the state or federal government.

Can be Tax-Deferred or Tax-Free – The income tax you pay will have a big impact on your available cash flow in retirement. That is why it is important that principal protected products be tax efficient, which you can get through both a tax-deferred and a tax-free investment.

Produce Rates of Return Between 5% and 12% - Up to this point, your money market accounts, savings accounts, and CDs would have qualified as principal protected, but unfortunately, I have ruled them out as a true principal protected product. These types of accounts are not going to produce the rates of return needed throughout your retirement to outpace inflation, which means they are subject to inflation risk.

There are only two products I have found that consistently meet these criteria – fixed indexed annuities and indexed universal life insurance. Since both may be critical in getting you to a risk-free retirement, I will cover both of them in detail in Chapter 13.

PRO TIP

Add principal protected products into your retirement plan to help you avoid sequence of return risk during the first five to ten years of retirement.

CHAPTER SEVEN

RISK #5: WITHDRAWAL RATE RISK

Withdrawal rate risk is the risk you will distribute your retirement assets too quickly and run out of assets before you run out of retirement.

MetLife conducted a retirement study back in 2008, and they asked people what an appropriate withdrawal rate in retirement would be. Of those who responded, 46% percent of them said 10% was an appropriate withdrawal rate. This is shocking to me. Even back in the mid-1990s, when both the stock and bond markets were performing as well as they ever had, William Bengen proved that with a withdrawal rate of only 5.5%, people were running out of money over 50% of the time.

Recent interest rates have been at historical lows. Most deposit accounts have been paying less than 1%, although they are finally going back up. This means those of you who got scared of the market and moved your assets into deposit accounts that were paying less than 1%, you only have about 11 years at a 10% distribution rate before you are broke. I do not know about you, but I am hoping my retirement assets will last longer than 11 years, especially when I consider my wife's age (she is four years younger than me) and my own life expectancy into the mix.

Financial planners have used a variety of ways to calculate what withdrawal rates should be, and there is one method that has come out as the winner for most advisors.

MONTE CARLO METHOD

Stanislaw (Stan) Ulam was a Polish mathematician who had moved to America and was working for the U.S. government during World War II. He worked as part of the team that had been hired to create the atomic and hydrogen bombs. At the end of the war, Stan suffered a brain injury and was unable to keep working. As the doctors assessed his situation, they told him they had both good and bad news regarding his condition. The good news was his brain would recover, and he would be healthy again. The bad news was they had no idea how long it was going to take before this happened.

To pass the time while he was recovering, Stan played solitaire. After a few months and hundreds of solitaire games, Stan's brain function started to return. As he was contemplating the outcomes of each game, Stan started putting together a complex math calculation he could use to determine the probable outcomes of each of his games. He was successful, and he called the formula the Monte Carlo Method after the gambling hot spot in Monaco where his uncle liked to visit.

Then in the mid-1990s, a financial advisor by the name of William Bengen decided to use the Monte Carlo Method to evaluate the withdrawal rates of retirement plans at the time, which most of them were using around a 7% withdrawal rate. He wanted to see if the plans could withstand such large withdrawals. What he found is even at a 5.5% withdrawal rate, over 50% of the plans were failing. After much testing, he finally concluded 4% was the correct amount, and he named his finding the Safemax rate, or what most advisors refer to as the 4% Rule.

The Monte Carlo Method has been used by financial planners for decades, but a lot has changed over the last twenty-plus years. Is 4% still a correct withdrawal rate? What the Monte Carlo Method has found is that 4% is too high for many retirees. A correct withdrawal rate using the Monte Carlo Method under current circumstances is closer to 3%, with some advisors believing the withdrawal rate should be as low as 2.5%. As easy as this may be to calculate for your retirement, the amount of money needed for your retirement can be difficult to accumulate. Here are several things you should consider when you are faced with such low withdrawal rates for your retirement.

Save More – Most of America could benefit from saving more for their retirement, but most will not because they have nothing left at the end of the month to save. We have succumbed to marketing agencies who want us to believe instant gratification is the only option to a successful and happy life when it is indeed the opposite. The more we delay our gratification and set money aside for our future, the more long-lasting joy and happiness we will have. A good way to increase your savings is to make it a priority. You can do this by making your savings one of the first bills you pay each month instead of the last. Depending on the age you start saving it may require you to save as little as 10% of your income, as much as 35% of your income, or anywhere in between.

Spend Less – Spending less goes together with saving more. For someone to be able to save more, they must have money they can save, which often means they must cut back on their spending to make extra money available. The best thing you can do here is to establish a budget you can stick with. A budget will help you keep on track with your financial goals.

Work Longer – Of all the things you can do to make up for a shortfall in your retirement savings, this might be the best option. Far too many people are hanging up their boots, aprons, and calculators earlier than they should. I realize work is hard. I realize your body may even be worn out. But I also realize securing retirement in your 60s is much easier than trying to save a retirement in your 80s. Continuing to work often provides three benefits. First, it may keep you from having to make a large spend-down of your assets during what would have been the early years of your retirement. Second, this additional work may provide you with extra money to save. Third, it will help keep your mind and body active.

If full-time work is no longer for you, consider part-time work or contract work. Many people have found doing some level of work in their retirement years helps them both monetarily and emotionally.

Die Sooner – I do not recommend this for anyone, nor do I see hands raised in live events when I ask if this were the option they would like to choose. But the reality is, this is one of the main ways people get out of living through decades of a less-than-ideal retirement. For some, health issues shorten their lives, for others, it is hereditary issues, and for a few, it is even accidents.

The problem is you do not know when you are going to die, so how do you plan for an uncertain life expectancy? You plan for a long retirement (up to age 100 or more), and if it does not work out for you to live this long, at least you did not have to experience the less-than-ideal retirement you may have faced during your later years had you not done the planning. I have been working with retirees now for almost three decades, and I can tell you I have never had anyone come back from the other side, including my parents, and complain they died too young and wish they had spent more money while they were alive. But I have had hundreds of individuals reach out to me that are now in their 80s and 90s that are broke and wish they had done things differently in the early years of their retirement.

Take More Risk – The last thing most people want to do with their retirement portfolio is to take more risk, but this has become a trend being promoted by many top advisors. The reason behind it seems to be because people are so far behind in their savings that they do not see any other possible way of catching up to where they need to be. You can see how this works in the following example.

Example: Ben is 60 and has $100,000 saved for his retirement. Based on the plan put together by his financial advisor, Ben needs about $400,000 at age 70 to help supplement his Social Security. Ben has been saving $6,000 a year and has been getting an average return rate of 6%.

Based on this information, Ben will be $141,830 short of his retirement goal. After further analysis, Ben learns he can meet his goal if he is willing to save an additional $12,000 a year. If Ben could discipline himself and save this extra money, he would have saved $416,339 by age 70. But what if Ben does not have any more money to save each year? He can take more risk and put his money into an investment paying 12%, and he will have $415,877 saved by age 70. In a world where instant gratification has become king, and we do not want to sacrifice any more than we must, you can see why Ben may be tempted to take the risk. It appears like an "I can have my cake and eat it too" situation.

For some, this method of investing is going to work out, but I do not recommend it. The reason is because there is a high probability taking the extra risk not only does not work out, but also destroys what savings you already have. When this happens, you may be sacrificing a less than ideal retirement for a Social Security only retirement.

A simple method for calculating a withdrawal rate is to take your age and divide it by 20. Example: 60 years/20 = 3%. 80 years/20 = 4%

PRO TIP

Use principal protected products to help you increase your withdrawal rate in retirement.

CHAPTER EIGHT

RISK #6: LONG-TERM CARE RISK

Long-term care risk is the risk you will become permanently disabled in retirement and require daily care by a third party and/or in a facility.

If you are like most people, you have spent your life trying to mitigate risk. Most of America has some form of homeowners insurance to protect them against a flood. Yet there is only a 3% chance you will ever need to use the insurance for this reason. If you have an automobile, chances are you have some type of automobile insurance to protect you against an accident that would total your car. Although I was shocked to learn about 20% of America is driving uninsured, so take that into consideration next time you are on the road. But for those of you who have auto insurance there is only an 18% chance you will ever total your car and use the insurance for this purpose. Yet you have a 35% chance you will become permanently disabled and be required to spend hundreds of thousands of dollars to take care of yourself and only 6% of you have a plan in place to cover a long-term event. You might be surprised to know that more of you (11%) believe in Bigfoot, the Boggy Creek Monster, Sasquatch, or whatever else you call him in your area, than have planned for a long-term care event. And I can give you a 100% guarantee you will never see Bigfoot, yet you believe. Statistics show that if you live to average life expectancy, you will have a 70% chance of having a long-term care event. This means there is a 35% chance anyone reading this book will become permanently disabled in retirement because half of us will be dead by the time we reach average life expectancy.

A long-term care event is when a doctor confirms you cannot do two of the six activities of daily living.
- **Eating**
- **Bathing**
- **Toileting**
- **Continence**
- **Transferring**
- **Dressing**

One of the biggest challenges with a long-term care event is Medicare will not be covering the cost of it, nor will any other health insurance you may be contracted with. Long-term care is the uncovered gap in the medical industry. Most of the services provided for long-term care events are provided by non-licensed professionals, which is why traditional health insurance companies like Medicare are not going to step in. You don't need a doctor to feed you oatmeal in the morning, or a nurse to help you put on your blouse or trousers. This leaves you trying to figure out how you are going to cover one of the biggest financial risks you may face in your lifetime.

Medicare only pays the following towards a long-term care event:

- 100% of the first 20 days (if you meet certain conditions)
- A coinsurance for the next 80 days

There are five options you can consider to cover the costs of a long-term care event. You can self-insure, you can rely on family members, you can buy long-term care insurance, you can buy a permanent life insurance policy with a no-fee chronic illness rider, or you can rely on Medicaid to bail you out.

Self-insure – This is where you take on the risk of paying for all the costs associated with a long-term care event. The biggest drawback if you decide to cover a long-term care event yourself is the cost. The cost of a private facility can be anywhere from about $6,000 a month on the low end to over $20,000 a month on the high end. The average long-term care stay for a male is 2.2 years, and for a female, it is 3.7 years, which means a long-term care event could end up costing you between $300,000 and $500,000, or more before it is over. Current estimates suggest that a married couple should have between $1,200,000 and $1,500,000 in assets if they plan to self-insure. Why would you need so much money, you ask? The biggest reason is because you should be saving for more than the long-term care event. You need to have assets left over after a long-term care event for the surviving spouse to live off, so they can maintain the lifestyle they enjoyed prior to the long-term care event. Remember, men, this responsibility lies primarily on you since you are usually the older spouse and have a shorter life expectancy.

If you are single, the estimated amount of money you should have saved for a long-term care event is between $300,000 and $500,000.

Another method some retirees are looking at to help pay for a long-term care event is a reverse mortgage. Reverse mortgages allow qualifying homeowners to borrow against the value of their home as either a lump sum, monthly installment, or a line of credit. The one rule most people overlook with a reverse mortgage as it relates to a long-term care event is the requirement that the home must be the primary residence of the borrower. If the borrower ends up in a long-term care facility for over 12 months, the long-term care facility is his new primary residence. Once this happens, the reverse mortgage will become due and payable. What I have found over the years is nobody wants to be trying to figure out how to sell their home at a time when they are dealing with the issues a long-term care event will bring about. Therefore, make sure you have done your homework and have a good plan to shelter in place, or have a spouse who can stay in the home, if you are considering a reverse mortgage to cover your long-term care. If you are married, both of you can be signers on the reverse mortgage (if you are both over age 62) to help reduce the chance of something like this happening.

Rely on Family Members – A quick look back in history reveals a time when many people considered family members as their best option for taking care of them during a long-term care event, but times have changed. The continued urbanization of America has many families spread out more than ever before, and many families are no longer built on a foundation of traditional family values, which means people are spending more time at work and have less available time to take care of their loved ones. In addition, for those family members who are available to offer care, there seems to be a growing level of resentment due to the amount of work and sacrifice that is required to take care of someone who cannot take care of themselves. This resentment is magnified when the children are the ones providing the care, and unfortunately, it comes with consequences. We are seeing a large percentage of children who must take care of an aging parent go through more complex mental struggles and divorce because of the strain such an event adds to their own life. There is nothing easy about taking care of an aging adult, making it quite easy for the stress, pressure, and time commitment to start affecting any family relationship. Please make sure you take all of this into consideration before asking a family member to perform such an arduous task. Since COVID, there have been more family members stepping in and taking care of their loved ones, but the trend is not expected to last.

Buy Long-Term Care Insurance – If you end up having a long-term care event, buying long-term care insurance is a much cheaper option than trying to self-insure, but what if you do not have a long-term care event and end up dying peacefully in your sleep at age 90 having never used the insurance you paid for? Most of you are going to get nothing in return, which is not something anyone gets very excited about.

Traditional long-term care insurance policies have several problems, but these policies can also provide many benefits when purchased correctly. I recommend you do the following if you are going to buy a long-term care insurance policy:

- Set your premium payments up over as short a period as possible. I recommend you buy a policy with a single payment, but if you cannot come up with this amount of money, I do not recommend going over ten years. My reason for this is because far too many people are getting policies that require a lifetime of payments only to find that when they need the insurance the most, they may not be able to keep up with the payments and must let the insurance lapse. You do not want to still be paying for the insurance at the time you are ready to make a claim. I had someone reach out to me who was experiencing this problem. He was 87 and his wife was 85, and they were finally at a point where they had a very high probability of needing their long-term insurance, but they were struggling to afford it. When they bought the policies back in 1993, the policies seemed very affordable. Now, 30 years later the total cost of their long-term care policies had increased to $37,000 a year and there was no death benefit or protection if they stopped paying the premiums. They were in between a rock and a hard spot you don't want to find yourself in. Premiums are also going up on these policies on a regular basis, so if you can get your premiums paid up, you will no longer be responsible for covering any future cost increases that the insurance company might have. This cost will be passed on to those individuals who are still making premium payments.

- The sooner you can buy long-term care insurance, the better. The cost of long-term care insurance is cheaper the younger you are when you buy it. This is why I recommend you purchase the insurance early on. The longer you wait, the more it will cost. You can buy a long-term care policy up until the age of 85, but I do not suggest waiting that long due to the high cost you will have to pay for the premiums.

- Consider pre-existing conditions. There is no pre-existing condition safety net with long-term care policies, so if you have a bad neck, bad back or are showing signs of cognitive decline, you might be unable to get a policy. If you do have pre-existing conditions, you may want to investigate a group policy through your employer. These policies usually do not require the applicants to go through underwriting.

- Get an inflation-adjusted policy. The cost of a long-term care event increases on an annual basis, so consider a policy with inflation-adjusted benefits.

- Consider one with a death benefit. This will keep you from losing all your money if you never have to use the insurance.

- Consider the other restrictions your policy might offer, such as the number of days the policy covers as well as the waiting periods after you have a long-term care event before benefits can start.

Permanent Life Insurance with a No-Fee Chronic Illness Rider – Recent innovations in the life insurance industry have opened the door for those who were looking for a better option to plan for a long-term care event. To improve the attractiveness of a permanent insurance policy during retirement, many life insurance companies have begun offering a no-fee chronic illness rider. This no-fee rider should not be confused with the paid long-term care rider many insurance companies also offer. The paid long-term care rider is often subpar to a standalone policy you could buy.

The no-fee chronic illness rider allows the insured to access a portion of the death benefit prior to death if they experience a long-term care event. It also takes away the worry of losing everything you have paid into a long-term care policy if you die peacefully in your sleep because there is a death benefit to the life insurance policy. The no-fee chronic illness rider will differ a little depending on your insurance carrier, but here are the basics of how using the chronic illness rider works.

Example: *Erica has an indexed universal life insurance policy with a $400,000 death benefit and a no-fee chronic illness rider (this option is not available with all life insurance policies and is not something you can add once you have purchased the policy). Erica just turned age 85 and is experiencing a long-term care event. She does not want to have to spend down her other assets to pay for the event, so she files a claim with her life insurance company to activate her chronic illness rider, which requires her to submit a letter from her doctor stating that she cannot perform two of the six activities of daily living. Based upon the terms of her policy, Erica gets immediate access to 24% of her death benefit, reduced to her age.* In this situation, Erica received $81,600 under the terms of her rider. Once paid, there are no restrictions on how Erica can spend this money. She can spend the money she receives on a private facility; she can spend it to pay family members who are helping her out, or she can spend it by sending the grandkids on a cruise.

Let us assume Erica is still struggling with long-term care issues a year later. She will notify the insurance company by completing the necessary documents, including an updated letter from her doctor. The insurance company will then provide her with an additional $81,600. For our example, let us assume by the next year, Erica will pass away. At this point, she has already received 48% of her available death benefit (reduced for early withdrawals), so her beneficiaries will receive the remaining 52%, or $208,000. The maximum number of years Erica can receive early distributions for a chronic illness is four, and if she were to die peacefully in her sleep, having never had a long-term care event, her beneficiaries would get the full $400,000 death benefit provided by the policy.

There are a few other benefits these life insurance policies have over traditional long-term care insurance you should know about as well. First, you do not have to worry about increasing premiums. Your insurance premiums will be set at the time your policy is purchased. Second, these policies are issued based on mortality, not morbidity, which means you do not have to worry about being uninsured if you have a bad neck or back - or any other health issue that may impact your daily life, but do not lead to an early death. Of all the options available, permanent life insurance with a chronic illness rider is my favorite for those who qualify.

Medicaid - If you fail to put together your own plan and need Medicaid to step in and cover the costs, please know it does not come without a price. For a married couple with only one spouse in a facility, Medicaid will only allow the other spouse to keep their own assets and income, one car, one house, up to $3715.50 a month in monthly maintenance needs allowance, and up to $148,600 in countable assets. If you are single, or both spouses are in a facility, you will only be able to keep around $2,000 in countable assets. The $2,000 you keep is to cover funeral costs. Medicaid is a state-run program in conjunction with the federal government which is why I have only provided "up to" and "around" amounts. If you want to better understand the spenddown rules for your state, please check out your state's Medicaid website. The spenddown rules I have provided are based upon general federal guidelines.

Medicaid also has a 60-month lookback period. They do this because they want to make sure you are not making them pay for services you could have paid for yourself had you not transferred assets you had available to pay for your care to related parties prior to signing up for assistance. This means if you transfer assets within 60-months of signing up for Medicaid to assist with paying for a long-term care event, you will not be able to get Medicaid assistance for a while. Medicaid determines the length of time you will be ineligible for benefits by taking the amount they would have paid to cover your care and dividing said amount into the amount of money that was transferred to related parties. The result is the number of months you will be ineligible for assistance. To help you better understand this concept let's look at an example.

Example: Johnny just turned 84 and his health is starting to fail. He is trying to come to grips with the reality that he may soon need someone to take care of him daily. As he reviews his financial situation, Johnny cannot help but be frustrated with the fact his chances of leaving his two daughters a legacy was now pretty much over. A long-term care event would eat up his remaining assets. Not understanding the five-year lookback period for Medicaid, Johnny decided to transfer $75,000 of his remaining cash to each of his two daughters. Six months after the transfer Johnny's health declined to where he could no longer do two of the six activities of daily living. His local senior center had recently provided him with information on Medicaid's role in a long-term care event, so he called the number they had provided to see if he could sign up for their assistance. The local Medicaid office provided Johnny with the necessary paperwork, and he started filling it out. One of the questions Johnny had to answer was, "Have you transferred any assets to a related party within the last five years?" Being the honest guy that he is, Johnny answered yes, and let Medicaid know he had recently transferred a total of $150,000 to his daughters. After reviewing his paperwork, his assigned Medicaid officer reached out to Johnny to let him know his application had been denied and he would not be eligible for any assistance from Medicaid at this time. The officer explained that he would have been eligible for $5,000 a month in benefits, but because of his transfer of assets to his daughters he would not be eligible for these benefits for 30 months (150,000/5,000 = 30). Johnny was told his best option would be to try and get this money back from his two daughters, but if he was unable to do this he may be in a state of disaster for his retirement since the government would not be stepping back in for another two and a half years.

As sad as this story is, it is happening consistently across America. Please do not think you can transfer money to your loved ones and then hide the transfer from the government either. Because if you get caught, you will have a warm place to stay and be fed three meals a day, but it will be in jail, not a nursing home.

LONGEVITY AND LONG-TERM CARE

Living to average life expectancy puts a retiree at a 70% chance of having a long-term care event. Medical and scientific breakthroughs have contributed to longer lives, but it does not always mean you will be living the life you want.

PRO TIP

Consider permanent life insurance with a no-fee chronic illness rider as an alternative to expensive long-term care insurance.

CHAPTER NINE

RISK #7: INFLATION RISK

Inflation risk is the risk that inflation will erode your buying power during retirement.

Many people refer to inflation as the silent killer of retirement because its impact is almost unrecognizable if you look at it daily. It isn't until you look at the impact of inflation over larger spans of time you realize how much it is hurting your overall retirement.

When you look back at the history of America, you will find that we have had periods of high inflation and we have had periods of deflation, but when we add all these together, the overall inflation rate has settled in at just under 3%. If you have 3% inflation and you are still working or own a business, the impact of inflation can usually be overcome. For those of you who are employees, there is a good chance you will get cost-of-living adjustments from your employer to offset the impact of inflation. For those of you who are self-employed, you will adjust your fees to your customers to make up for inflation. But what happens when you get to retirement and the only inflation-adjusted income you have is your Social Security? If there is inflation, your fixed income will buy fewer goods and services each year. The easiest way to calculate the estimated impact of inflation on your retirement is to use the Rule of 72 but in reverse.

The Rule of 72 has been used for decades by financial advisors to show their clients how fast their money will double. The calculation is simple. Take the expected rate of return and divide it into 72. The result is the approximate number of years it will take for available assets to double.

Example: Larry has $100,000 and is estimating an 8% rate of return. How long will it take for Larry to double his money? Divide 8 into 72, and you get 9. With an 8% return rate, Larry will be able to turn his $100,000 into $200,000 within about 9 years.

Now let's reverse the calculation, using the inflation rate rather than the expected rate of return, and see how much buying power Larry will lose over time due to inflation. The calculation is designed to estimate how long it will take to lose half the buying power of the assets you currently have.

Example: Larry has $100,000 and is estimating a 3% inflation rate. How long will it take for his spending power to be cut in half? Divide 3 into 72, and you get 24. This means within 24 years the buying power of Larry's $100,000 will only be about $50,000.

PRO TIP

Find assets you can invest in that outpace inflation.

CHAPTER TEN

RISK #8: MEDICARE RISK

Medicare risk is the risk you will not sign up for Medicare at the appropriate time and for the appropriate benefits, and end up having to pay thousands of dollars in medical costs you would not be responsible for had you signed up for Medicare correctly in the first place.

Most people think signing up for Medicare is a simple two-step process. Turn 65 and fill out some paperwork. I wish I could say the process was this easy, but it is not. Medicare is an overly complex health insurance program – with some major conse-quences if you get it wrong. Since it is my goal to help you tran-sition into retirement with as little pain as possible, I will cover some of the consequences.

Liable for what Medicare should have paid – When you are dealing with more than one insurance company, you have what is called primary and secondary insurer. The primary insurer is the insurance company responsible for paying for your medical costs first and covering your care up to your insurance limits with the company. The secondary insurer steps in after the primary insured has paid what they are responsible for and then pays most, if not all, of the costs that are remaining. If you choose not to sign up for Medicare at age 65, you might become your own primary insurer. This happens when you are covered by small employer health coverage (fewer than 20 full-time or part-time employees), and you choose not to sign up for Medicare at age 65. The problem here is your small employer's coverage goes from being your primary insurer to the secondary insurer once you turn 65. This means if you do not sign up for Medicare and you have a major medical event, your small employer coverage will not step in until you have paid out of your own pocket all the costs Medicare would have paid as your primary insurer.

Increase in premiums – If you miss your optimal enrollment and you do not have creditable coverage, Medicare will charge you a 10% per year penalty on your Part B insurance for each year you do not sign up for coverage. This penalty must be paid for the rest of your life. Let's look at an example of how this works.

Example: Jeanette was in good health at age 65, so she did not feel it was necessary to sign up for Medicare since she would be stuck paying Part B premiums she may never get any benefit out of. She is now 70 years old and has enjoyed years of good health, but decides she better not push her luck any further. She goes online to sign up for Medicare. What she finds is not only will she need to pay her regular Part B premiums, but she must also pay a 50% surcharge on this premium for the rest of her life (10% times the five years she was uninsured).

The reason Medicare charges this penalty is because Medicare works like every other health insurance company – the healthy people cover the costs for the unhealthy people. Therefore, Medicare has implemented this penalty to keep people from waiting to sign up for Medicare until their health gets to a point where it will benefit them to sign up. There is also a 1% per month penalty for Part D benefits if you go without creditable coverage for a period of 63 days. Creditable coverage is different for Part B and Part D. The best way to learn whether you have creditable coverage or not is to talk with your current insurance provider.

Missed Medigap guarantee period – The Medigap guarantee period is a six-month period which begins the month you turn 65 and are enrolled in Medicare Part B. During the Medigap guarantee period, insurance companies are prohibited from denying coverage or overcharging you for a Medigap policy, regardless of pre-existing health conditions. By law, all beneficiaries are protected from unfair medical underwriting, and these protections exist to oversee this. If you miss your open enrollment period, you can also buy a Medigap policy when you have a guaranteed issue right, but you may pay more or not be able to get access to all policies offered by an insurance company.

You may have a guaranteed issue right if:
- You, through no fault of your own, lost a group health plan (GHP) that covered your Medicare cost-sharing (meaning it paid secondary to Medicare)
- You joined a Medicare Advantage Plan when you first became eligible for Medicare and disenrolled within 12 months

- Or your previous Medigap policy, Medicare Advantage Plan, or PACE program ends its coverage or commits fraud

Note: If you have a Medicare Advantage Plan, Medicare SELECT policy, or PACE program and you move out of the plan's service area, you also have the right to buy a Medigap policy.

Be sure to keep a copy of any letters, notices, postmarked envelopes, and claim denials in case you need proof that you lost or ended health coverage. Medigap insurers may require these documents before they sell you a policy.

Some issues you might run into if you try to buy a Medigap policy outside a protected enrollment period include companies can refuse to sell you a policy or impose certain medical requirements to qualify. And even if a company does agree to sell you a policy, you may be required to pay a higher monthly premium and be subject to a six-month waiting period before the Medigap policy will cover pre-existing conditions. If you are worried about ending up in this position, or you are already in this position, you can reach out to Medigap insurers in your state to learn if they will sell you a Medigap policy outside protected enrollment periods and what the cost would be.

Gap in coverage – Medicare works very much like current marketplace insurance. There are certain available enrollment periods, and if you miss them, you will not be able to sign up until the next available enrollment period. This means you may have a gap in your coverage that could last as long as 15 months. If you miss your eligible enrollment period, you will not be able to sign up for Medicare until the general enrollment period that opens up each year from January 1st to March 31st. The biggest problem with this is even once you have signed up for Medicare you will still have to wait until July 1st to get coverage.

Larger out-of-pocket costs – I talked about one of the issues with this earlier with primary and secondary insurance, but there is a second issue. If you end up being denied a Medigap policy due to missing an enrollment window, then the policy you can get may have higher deductibles and larger co-pays.

Loss of freedom to choose – Nobody wants to lose their freedom to choose, but this might be exactly what happens to you if you miss your optimal enrollment period. You will find yourself stuck abiding by the rules of the Medicare program to tell you what you can do with Medicare and when.

The best way to solve Medicare risk is to start doing your homework on the program and then connecting with a Medicare broker who can guide you to success. I recommend you get started on your homework by going to www.medicare.gov. Here you will find educational resources as well as information to compare available Medigap and Medicare Advantage Plan in your area. Most people will sign up for Medicare during the initial enrollment period which starts three months before your 65th birth month and goes until three months after your 65th birth month. There are also special enrollment periods those with creditable coverage after age 65 often enroll during.

MEDICARE OPTIONS

Original Medicare (Part A and B) – Original Medicare, or what is sometimes called traditional Medicare, consists of Medicare Part A and Part B. Medicare Part A is hospitalization insurance and is free for most of you. Medicare Part B is your standard health insurance and requires you to pay a monthly premium. Both Part A and Part B will be extremely helpful in covering your medical costs during retirement, but there are gaps in coverage in both parts. Once you sign up for original Medicare, you will get access to a variety of options to help you cover the gaps that exist in the program. These gaps include co-pays, co-insurance, and deductibles.

Medicare Part C - Medicare Advantage Plans (MAP) – Medicare Part C is provided by third-party insurance companies. To join a Medicare Advantage Plan, you must have Medicare Part A and B and live in the plan's service area. A Medicare Advantage Plan will provide your Medicare Part A and Part B coverage, plus provide other benefits. These plans are becoming more popular by the day, but they are not a perfect fit for everyone. Some of the main concerns retirees have with these plans are the lack of benefits if you are outside the plan's coverage area, the ability to only see doctors who are in your plan's network, and the need to get pre-approval to see a specialist.

If you decide to go with a Medicare Advantage Plan, you will have many options to choose from:

- Health Maintenance Organization (HMO)
- Preferred Provider Organization (PPO)
- Private Fee-for-Service Plan (PFFS)
- Special Needs Plan (SNP)
- HMO Point-of-Service (HMOPOS)
- Medical Savings Accounts (MSA)

What you pay will be based upon the plan you choose and the insurance company you go with. There are many MAPs that are no-fee plans. This means you do not pay anything to the insurance company for the additional benefits that the plan provides.

PRO TIP

If you sign-up for a Medicare Advantage Plan, do not stop paying your Part B premiums. You must continue to pay these premiums, or the government will lapse your coverage.

Medicare Part D – Medicare Part D is a federal program that began in 2006. It provides Medicare beneficiaries with access to retail prescription drugs at affordable co-pays. This voluntary program allows you to access medications at a more affordable rate. It also provides insurance against catastrophic drug costs. Third-party insurance companies provide the prescription drug benefits. Prior to 2006, people on Medicare usually paid out-of-pocket for their medications.

Medicare Supplement Plan (Medigap) – If you are looking for the best coverage with the most freedom, then you will want to consider a Medigap policy, or what is often referred to as a Medicare supplement policy. A Medigap policy is an insurance policy provided by a third-party insurance company that helps supplement original Medicare. A Medigap policy can help pay most of the remaining health care costs that the original Medicare does not. Some of the things a Medigap policy may pay for are co-payments, co-insurance, and deductibles. Original Medicare pays for much, but not all, of the cost of covered health care services and supplies.

There has been a total of twelve different Medigap plans available over the years, but currently, only eight of them are being sold – A, B, D, G, K, L, M, and N. The government wanted to ensure that those buying these policies had skin in the game, so even the best plan now requires you to at least pay your annual Part B deductible if you have medical issues and use the insurance.

CHAPTER ELEVEN

RISK #9: ELDER FINANCIAL ABUSE RISK

Elder financial abuse risk is the risk of financial exploitation after age 60.

If you have spent much time watching the news or looked up the news online, you probably have seen a story where someone has gotten conned out of a substantial amount of money. And you may have thought to yourself, "How could they be so stupid? There is no way I would fall for something like that." Yet social media and news outlets share stories on a regular basis of people who got taken advantage of that never thought it could happen to them, including my in-laws.

My in-laws were both over age 60 and had been contemplating their retirement for a few years. One day I was busy working when I got a call from my father-in-law asking me if I could help them with a financial issue they were dealing with. My father-in-law is a professional cabinet maker, and I had been doing accounting and tax work for them over the years, so I assumed he was calling to ask about the business. Unfortunately, I soon found out he was not calling about the business but a major problem they had with their retirement funds.

Prior to this phone call, I did not know all of the details of my in-law's retirement situation. What I did know is they did not have the money they needed to retire with the same lifestyle they were currently living. My in-laws had struggled financially for their whole life. My father-in-law is amazing at what he does, but he could never bring himself to charge his customers for the value of what his product was worth. This meant that his family always got left on the short end of the financial stick. My mother-in-law spent most of her life raising kids and dealing with the side effects of depression and a lifetime of prescription drug abuse, so she had never been able to provide much towards the family finances either. All of this meant my in-laws were walking into their retirement with very little money to get through safely. My father-in-law's business was about the only thing they had of any value.

As I contemplated what I already knew, my father-in-law started explaining what the issue was he needed help with. He explained how my mother-in-law had always hated the fact that she was unable to provide more financial resources for the family. So, now that the kids were out of the house, she thought things could be different. With the spare time she now had, my mother-in-law started looking for ways she could add financial value to their upcoming retirement. As she was searching online for opportunities, she came across an ad about starting an online drop ship store. The ad talked about how easy it was to start and how they could teach anyone how to do it. As she got further into the ad, my mother-in-law thought to herself, "This is just what I have been looking for. I can finally get my husband out of the cabinet shop. I can bring in enough money with this business to supplement our Social Security right out of our own home." She took the bait.

Long story short, by the time this company was done with her, my mother-in-law not only had one online store that was going nowhere, but she also had three other online stores that were going nowhere. She was the proud owner of four new limited liability companies. She had coaching calls available to her for the next year. She even paid in advance to have the tax returns prepared for all her entities, which I found very strange since, up to this point, I had been helping them file all their tax returns, and I had been willing to do it for free.

As my father-in-law further explained the situation, he proceeded to tell me how his wife had used not only all their savings to pay for these start-up businesses, but she had also maxed out their credit cards and was now starting to add to their home equity line. You can imagine how devastated he was when he learned what was previously looking like a not-so-great retirement was now looking like a will never happen retirement. He explained how the company that had placed the ad and their affiliates had been paid over $50,000 by my mother-in-law before he stumbled onto what was happening and was able to put a stop to it.

Once my father-in-law had me updated on all the facts, he asked if there was anything I could do to help them get out of the situation. Knowing my mother-in-law as I did, I realized she had two things going for her I should be able to use to help them. First, she was over age 60, so everything she went through with these various companies could be considered elder abuse. Second, she was not even in a mental state to be able to understand what she bought, let alone be able to run a business.

I went to work. I got the financial records from my in-laws so I could see who got what money. I called the state of Utah's elder abuse line to get some additional information on the laws I was uncertain about. I then reached out to each of these companies, letting them know they had committed elder abuse and asked them for the money back. By the time I was done, I had been able to get over 90% of the money back and had been able to help them keep the small amount of money they had for their retirement.

Unfortunately, most elder abuse scams do not come up with this good of an ending. Retirees across the country are having their retirements destroyed by unscrupulous people, and your retirement may be the next one on their list. As you age, many things happen that make it easier for those with bad intentions to take advantage of you.

Here are a few of the big ones:

- There are times of loneliness, making it easy to mistake a scam for friendship
- Your brain may stop working at the level it used to
- You may have more money than you have ever had, which makes you a target
- You may not have others to bounce ideas off as you did during your working years.

Any one of these by itself can be problematic, but if you start stacking these items on top of each other, you start to better understand why so many retirees are subject to elder financial abuse.

PRO TIP

If you would like to learn more about elder abuse and find out what resources are available to help you if you have been subject to elder abuse, go to www.olderadultnestegg.com.

SIGNS OF ELDER FINANCIAL ABUSE

Elder financial abuse generally does not happen overnight, but since most retirees will never admit they have been abused until it is too late, there are some signs you should look for when trying to identify abuse to a family member or friend.

A change in address for financial documents – If you are someone who was receiving financial documents for a loved one who is in retirement and suddenly you aren't anymore and you do not know why, or if you notice financial documents at a loved one's home and the address on them is no longer their address, this could be a sign of elder financial abuse.

Fraudulent signatures on documents – Financial documents should be reviewed on a regular basis. This includes looking at checks and credit card transactions for possible fraudulent signatures. If you find fraudulent signatures, you will need to try to uncover the extent of the fraud in hopes of getting recourse.

Missing belongings or property – Did grandma and grandpa use to have gold coins, jewelry, or other collectible items that are valuable, but now they are nowhere to be found? This could be a sign there is a problem. These are easy items for someone to take without you even noticing they are missing many times. These items should always be protected under lock and key, including often from family members, and the following story will illustrate the importance of this.

After my mom was diagnosed with cancer, there was a time it did not look like she was going to make it. This period of uncertainty led to questions about what would happen if my mom were to pass away. How would my dad survive financially? Who would take care of the three of us children who were still at home? Who would get some of mom's stuff my dad did not want? It also led to an opportunity for my oldest sister to potentially get her hands on a few items she had wanted for years.

The only two things my mom had of any monetary value at this time were her wedding ring, which was given to my wife years later by my mom, and some Madame Alexander dolls which at the time (1982) were worth over a hundred dollars each. The dolls were kept in my mom's unlocked cedar chest, and everyone in the family knew this, including my oldest sister. Knowing that if my mom passed away there could be a fight amongst my sisters over the dolls, my oldest sister decided to remove the risk. She opened the cedar chest, pulled out each doll, and then attached a piece of tape with her name on it to the top of each box. By adding this piece of tape, my sister hoped she would be able to show it was my mom's wish she received the dolls if my mom happened to pass away.

You can imagine my sister's surprise when shortly after my mom recovered from her cancer, she decided to go through her cedar chest. In the process my mom found the dolls with my sister's name still taped on each box. It was not a pleasant discussion for my sister to try and explain what happened since my mom recognized her handwriting. I have never felt it was right to talk to my sister about this experience, but I'm sure being so shortsighted is something she has regretted doing ever since.

Unpaid bills – This is usually one of the first signs of financial problems. If rather than seeing ads and letters from kids and grandkids on the counter, you start seeing stacks of bills, this is a sign that there may be financial issues.

Unusual activity or sudden changes in spending patterns – Most people are consistent in the way they live and the way they spend their time and money. If grandpa, who has always been out and active, now never leaves the house; or if your friend who used to meet you for lunch and a walk around the park is now only showing up for the walk around the park, this could be a sign there has been elder financial abuse.

The problem with elder abuse is that all the signs I have just mentioned are also signs of someone running out of money. Because of this there will often be a need to do more digging if you start seeing these signs with those you love and are responsible for.

STOPPING ELDER FINANCIAL ABUSE

The best way to eliminate the consequences of elder financial abuse is to prevent it from happening in the first place. Here are some things you can do for yourself and those you love to help stop the abuse.

Approach the issue as a family – Every family should have a family meeting at least annually. This meeting should cover a variety of issues facing your family, including finances. This can be a wonderful time to find out if there are any upcoming financial concerns, so you can be proactive rather than reactive.

Monitor your accounts – Regularly check activity and status on credit cards, bank statements, and your credit score. There are many companies you can pay to help you monitor for fraud or identity theft.

Simplify your retirement – Of all the things one can do to prevent elder financial abuse, this has proven to be the best option. When retirees have a simple plan they can follow and rely upon it, the chances for abuse are reduced substantially. It is important you try to convert, condense, and consolidate assets as much as you can.

Keep updated on current scams – A good place to find this information in retirement is AARP. They do an excellent job of keeping an updated list of scams and what to look for.

Keep a social connection – The pandemic is over, and it is time to get out and mingle! Look for opportunities to go to lunch, dinner or other social activities with friends and family. It is nice to talk on the phone or to receive a text, but nothing can replace face-to-face interaction.

Be sensitive when addressing elder financial abuse with your loved ones. If elder financial abuse has happened, most people will be very reluctant to talk about it due to embarrassment and the hope they can fix the problem themselves.

PRO TIP

A well-planned retirement will reduce your chances of falling subject to elder financial abuse. The problem with elder financial abuse is the average victim will lose over $100,000 to the abuser.

CHAPTER TWELVE

RISK #10: LACK OF INCOME DIVERSITY RISK

This is the risk you will not have enough income diversity to allow you to overcome all the financial risks facing your retirement.

If you are anything like me, you couldn't wait to receive your first paycheck from your job as a teenager. It may have been the first time you received financial recognition for all your hard work, above and beyond the room and board your parents had provided for doing your chores. Then you received your second check, your third check, your fourth check, and then you probably stopped counting because you realized what you had going was a pretty good gig because it was able to repeat itself monthly. You loved the consistency of being able to fill the bank account up each month with paychecks and then know you could spend the account down to pay your monthly bills. For many of you this process is all you ever wanted during your working years. Then you hit retirement, the one time in your life where a monthly check makes the most sense. Instead of using your retirement assets to create a monthly income you invest them into assets that have no guarantees, leaving you with Social Security as your only source of guaranteed income. I will never understand why we do this, but this is happening across the country.

Most of us learned about asset diversity in our first finance class in high school or college and its importance in protecting our overall investments. But very few people have ever heard anything about the importance of income diversity in retirement. The problem lack of income diversity causes is it doesn't allow us to spread out our retirement income into enough buckets to prevent us from being subject to many of the other risks I cover in this book. There are many options we can look at for income diversity in retirement, but if we also want to eliminate tax-rate risk we need to make sure all of our income sources are coming from the tax-free bucket.

RETIREMENT IS ABOUT INCOME

During retirement, many retirees choose to move to states from where they spent most of their working years. The move may be because of taxes, it may be because of weather, or it may be because they are trying to follow the kids. Regardless of the reason, I have found that nobody calls up the city office of the place they will be moving to ask, "How many assets will I need to be able to live in your city?" In fact, they are not calling anyone up and asking this question. It seems absurd just saying it. But there will be many people reaching out to cities, friends, and contacts on social media to find out how much income they will need to live in each area during retirement. They will want to know what the utility costs are. They will want to understand what the taxes are. How expensive is food and gas? These questions all make sense because we have spent decades asking these questions, so why would we expect them to change once we get into retirement?

TAX-FREE INCOME STREAMS

Tax-free income has been an afterthought for most retirees. Even once Roth accounts were introduced in 1997 as the end all be all for tax-free investing only about 5% of retirement assets have been contributed to these types of accounts. But times are changing as I have pointed out throughout this book. Therefore, if you are serious about getting to a risk-free retirement you will need to consider the following sources of tax-free income.

Roth IRA – When it comes to creating tax-free income in retirement one of the simplest things you can use is a Roth IRA. Not only do Roth accounts allow for tax-free growth, but they also allow for tax-free distributions. But as you can imagine, any good news from the government is usually followed by some unwelcome news, and Roth IRAs are no exception. Roth IRAs have two imposed limits that can be problematic for those trying to use these accounts for their retirement. First, they have income limits. If you have no "qualified" earned income, you will not be able to contribute, and if your modified adjusted gross income (MAGI) is too high, you will not be able to contribute. The MAGI limit changes each year and differs by filing status. I suggest you do an internet search for current income thresholds to learn what this limit will be for you.

Second, Roth IRAs are subject to contribution limits. The maximum amount you can contribute to a Roth IRA if you are under age 50 in 2023, is $6,500. If you are age 50 or older, the catch-up contribution is $1,000. As you can see, with these low limits, you may find it hard to save enough money to cover your retirement with only a Roth IRA.

Roth 401(k) – If you are lucky enough to have access to a Roth 401(k), you have access to what I believe is one of the best investment tools available for retirement. To me, they are even better than Roth IRAs. What are some things that make Roth 401(k)s such a great investment?

- They usually offer an employer match
- They do not have the income restrictions of an IRA
- They have higher contribution limits than an IRA

The contribution limit for 2023 is $22,500 for those under age 50, and there is a $7,500 catch-up contribution for those aged 50 or older.

Roth Conversions – When you belong to a society that has spent decades putting most of their retirement money into tax-deferred accounts, then they start realizing tax rates may be much higher for them in the future than they are today, what you get is a whole lot of Roth conversions. Simply put, Roth conversions are when you move money from a traditional retirement account into a Roth account. Because of this you can move funds from a traditional IRA into a Roth IRA or even rollover a traditional 401(k) into a Roth IRA. You will have to pay taxes on the money transferred over, but this means when you go to make withdrawals from the Roth account in the future you will not have to pay taxes on that amount. Roth conversions are happening at a rate that has not been seen in the history of America. People have come to realize they have until January 1, 2026, before taxes are scheduled to go up, and they do not want to miss this once in a lifetime opportunity. It is not every day we know what tax rates will be this far in advance.

Since I know many of you are part of the group who are doing Roth conversions, here are a few things to remember. First, do not try to convert all your assets in one year. This could easily subject you to much higher taxes today than you may be subject to in the future. Second, make sure you have enough money outside of your retirement accounts to pay the federal, state, and local government their share of the conversion if you are under age 59 ½. There is no need to subject yourself to the early withdrawal penalty. Third, there are currently no restrictions on who can do Roth conversions, how much you can convert, and when during the year they can be done, so plan accordingly.

Roth Annuities – If you love Social Security, you are going to love Roth annuities even better. Roth annuities have become a game changer for retirees because it allows them to enjoy the lifetime income benefits of an annuity in a tax-free environment. Thanks to recent changes by a handful of insurance companies, you now have two options on how you structure a Roth annuity. First, you can continue to do what has been done since the late 1990s and buy the annuity inside your Roth account. This option works well for those of you who have invested enough money into your Roth to buy the size of annuity needed to supplement your Social Security income. Second is to take advantage of the recent changes by a handful of forward-thinking insurance companies. Buy the annuity in a tax-deferred account and then slowly convert the annuity into your Roth account over time. This is what the industry calls an internal Roth conversion. This will allow you to better manage tax rate risk during the conversion period. The only rule you need to keep your eye on is the conversion must be completed prior to the annuity being annuitized.

Life Insurance Retirement Fund - I will talk in detail about this product in Chapter 13. For now, you should know the correct permanent life insurance policy is a great source of tax-free income you can use to help remove some risks from your retirement you may find impossible to remove without it.

Tax-Deferred Assets – You may be asking yourself, "How can a tax-deferred asset create tax-free income?" Because of the standard deduction the IRS allows us to use on our annual tax return. It is my belief the standard deduction is here to stay. If I am right, you can get a double win from the IRS on your tax-deferred assets if you put together the right plan. Because your original contribution to the account was tax-deferred, you did not have to pay tax on the money when you put it in, and if your distributions, along with any other taxable income you have, are lower than the annual standard deduction, you will not pay taxes when you pull the money out either. What a generous gift from our government.

The income created by your tax-deferred assets should also be low enough not to create provisional income, which will cause your Social Security to be taxed. In Chapter 14, when I lay out my Five Strategies for Getting Safely Through Retirement, I will further explain how much money you should have in your tax-deferred bucket once you retire. You may be excited to learn there is a mathematically correct amount you should have in your tax-deferred bucket based on your facts and circumstances.

Social Security – Around 40% of those receiving Social Security will pay tax on their benefits, but you may not have to be one of them. Through appropriate planning, you may be able to get your provisional income to a level where your Social Security will not be taxed during retirement. It will take work and some planning, but if you can get tax-free Social Security, you will be glad you did.

You can have millions of dollars of assets in retirement, but if you do not have income from these assets, you will have financial issues. When you get to retirement, you will need to switch your focus from asset diversity to income diversity. The more diverse your retirement income is, the better chance you have of managing the financial risks facing your retirement.

CHAPTER THIRTEEN

THE ROLE OF LIFE INSURANCE COMPANIES IN RETIREMENT PLANNING

For many of you, life insurance companies are the last people you want helping you out with your retirement. But if you are serious about eliminating the financial risks facing your retirement, you will find it near impossible to remove all the risks without using products insurance companies sell. Why? Because insurance companies were created to identify, reduce, and eliminate risk. When it comes to your retirement, there are two main products insurance companies offer that I recommend you consider: fixed indexed annuities and indexed universal life insurance. Why do I like these two products so much? Because they both meet all the qualifications of a principal protected product as explained in Chapter 6.

YUCK, ANNUITIES

When I mention annuities in a meeting or webinar, I often find that many people have a lot of negative opinions about them.

Many people even have horror stories to tell about how an annuity turned into a financial disaster. But as I ask more questions about why people feel the way they do, I soon find consistency in the responses. Most people have had issues with high-fee variable annuities. These high-fee variable annuities are tied to the stock market, so if the market takes a dip, the annuity goes with it. Which is exactly what happened to those of you who had variable annuities during some of the market's biggest crashes. If you had a variable annuity during the market downturns in 1987, 2000, 2008, or 2022, chances are you lost a large chunk of your annuity value. And to top it off, you may have been charged up to a 5% asset charge for the pleasure of losing all this money. I must admit, I would be upset, too.

What you need to remember, though, is variable annuities are not the only annuity available. Insurance companies have made some huge progress in their annuity products over the last decade. One of the products that has made a significant impact in helping to secure retirement plans across the county is the fixed indexed annuity.

FIXED INDEXED ANNUITIES WORK DIFFERENTLY THAN THE ANNUITIES OF THE PAST

When it comes to considering annuities for your retirement do not let the past scare you. Instead use it to motivate you to better understand how these products work. Let me share a few of the things I really like about fixed indexed annuities that make them different than other annuities you could buy. Which is why I already have three of them for my retirement!

- Fixed indexed annuities will provide guaranteed lifetime income no matter how long you live. There are two phases to an annuity contract. The accumulation phase, which is the period you are putting money into the annuity. And the distribution phase, the period you are taking money out of the annuity. During the accumulation phase there is a minimum guarantee and a projected amount you will receive once you annuitize the product. Once you get into the distribution phase whatever amount the insurance company calculates based upon the terms of your policy is what you will get each year for the rest of your life. No matter how long you live. You might also be excited to know there are some new annuities on the market that will allow your payout to increase each year or every other year if there is an increase in the index you chose after you annuitize the product.

- Instead of the money inside these products being invested directly into the stock market, the money is invested in options that are tied to indexes offered by the insurance company. By investing in these options, the annuity owner can get a portion of the upside growth if the index the annuity is invested in goes up because the insurance company will exercise the option. But the option protects the annuity owner from losing money if the index goes down because the insurance company will just let the option lapse. If the option is allowed to lapse, the annuity owner will be able to keep everything they had in the account before the loss in the index. This means if the index is down 20% the worst the indexed annuity owner will do is 0%.

- Almost all fixed indexed annuity products are spread products, not fee products. This means the high fees people used to pay to have variable annuities do not exist in these annuities. The annual fee the annuity owner will be charged on most fixed indexed annuities will be zero.

- There is a death benefit. This means if you were to pass away after you annuitized the annuity but before getting back your original investment, your beneficiaries would be paid out at least the difference between what you have already received and the amount you originally contributed. Some insurance companies will guarantee more than two times the original contribution. Each fixed indexed annuity is structured a little bit different, but this change has helped many people overcome the anxiety they have had regarding annuities and premature death. Traditional annuities were primarily structured as single premium immediate annuities (SPIA). This meant you turned over a bunch of money to an insurance company in the form of a single premium, and the insurance company would provide you with a guarantee you would get a monthly income for as long as you lived. If you lived to be 100, your annuity turned into a great investment that you were glad you bought. But what if you died two months after you signed up for your annuity, only having received a couple of checks? You lost. You ended up giving away a large amount of your retirement savings for a ridiculously small return. Current fixed indexed annuities provide an opportunity for your beneficiaries to get your capital investment back, so this huge loss of assets no longer happens.

- You can establish your fixed indexed annuity to where the income is tax-free. I talked about how this can be done back in Chapter 12 when I was talking about Roth annuities.

PERMANENT LIFE INSURANCE

In addition to annuities, insurance companies also offer a variety of permanent insurance products many people use to secure their retirement. And when you consider the benefits these products offer, you start realizing why these policies are considered the best loophole in the IRS code. These policies offer benefits you cannot find in any other investment.

1. **No early withdrawal penalties if you take money out before age 59 ½.** The way you get money out of a permanent insurance policy is by taking a loan against your cash value. Since the money you are taking out is a loan, there is no early withdrawal penalty as you would have with traditional retirement accounts. This can be a huge benefit, especially for those who want to retire early.

2. **Tax-free growth.** The income in these accounts will grow tax-free if you do not turn the policy into a modified endowment contract (MEC). In simple terms, it means you do not overfund the policy by turning it into a full-fledged investment rather than an insurance product. Insurance companies are on your side with this one. They will only accept and apply to your account the maximum premium your policy allows without turning it into a MEC, and not a penny more. If you pay in more to the insurance com-

pany than your policy allows, they will send you a letter notifying you have over-contributed. This letter will also inform you that if you want to turn your policy into a MEC by having them post this payment you must send back a notarized statement confirming your intent.

3. **Tax-free distributions.** Make sure you have one dollar of cash value left in the policy when you pass away, and all the money you take out of the policy during your lifetime will be tax-free. The best way to ensure this happens is to include an over-loan protection rider when you purchase your policy. This rider requires the insurance company to monitor all distributions you take during your lifetime from your insurance policy to make sure you do not lapse your policy by taking out too much money. If you get to a point where this is going to be a problem, the insurance company will cut off all future distributions to you.

4. **No income limits.** One of the problems many people have with Roth accounts is if you make too much money, you cannot contribute, and if you make too little money, you cannot contribute. With permanent life insurance policies, you can earn as much or as little as you want and still contribute.

5. **No contributions limit.** This does not mean you can put 100% of your money into these policies. But you do have the freedom to put as much or as little as you can afford into these policies. You can put a few hundred dollars a month into these policies or thousands of dollars a year into these policies, and you will still be able to qualify for the other benefits these policies offer.

6. **No legislative risk.** History speaks for itself. In 1982, the government passed the Tax Equity and Fiscal Responsibility Act (TEFRA). In 1984, they passed the Deficit Reduction Act (DEFRA), and in 1988 they passed the Technical and Miscellaneous Revenue Act (TAMRA). Each one of these acts changed the way permanent insurance policies worked, but each time the government grandfathered in everyone who had permanent insurance policies before the changes were made. There is no reason to assume that the same grandfathering rules will not apply to any future changes.

As you can see, there are several benefits a permanent insurance policy can offer you cannot find in any other investment.

WHAT TYPE OF PERMANENT INSURANCE POLICIES ARE AVAILABLE?

There are three main types of permanent insurance most people buy. Whole life insurance, variable life insurance, and universal life insurance. Universal life insurance is broken down into three categories – variable universal life insurance, universal life insurance and indexed universal life insurance. I will cover these various policies in more detail next when I cover the requirements you should look for in a permanent insurance policy.

ALL PERMANENT INSURANCE POLICIES ARE NOT CREATED EQUAL

To make your life insurance policy work the way it should, here is a list of things the policy should have:

- Safe and Productive Growth
- Low Fees
- Cost Free and Tax-Free Distributions
- Cost Free Chronic Illness Rider

Unfortunately, even many top insurance companies do not offer permanent life insurance products that include all the items on this list.

Safe and productive growth: Whole life policies are safe, but they are not very productive — current whole life policies are not even keeping up with inflation. Whole life policies offer a guaranteed death benefit and a guaranteed cash value growth, but these benefits come at a cost. Whole life policies will cost you more for the insurance and they will not provide the productive growth you need if you are hoping to use your life insurance as a retirement vehicle. Variable life insurance, variable universal life insurance, and universal life insurance policies are productive, but they are not very safe – these policies often get destroyed when there is a downturn in the market. These policies work very similar to variable annuities, only the insurance policy comes with a death benefit. This leaves us with an indexed universal life policy as our best option. Because you get the benefits of upside growth in the stock market without any downturn risk.

I experienced the pain volatility can cause from a variable life insurance policy firsthand back in the late 1990s and early 2000s. I was in my late 20s, and unfortunately, I did not know then what I know now. So, when a friend showed me an illustration for a very high performing variable life insurance policy, I saw it as a good opportunity to protect my family. My friend had ran the illustration at 12%, which he claimed was a safe rate to run the illustration since the technology boom at the time I purchased the policy was creating rates of return in some accounts of over 100%. I bought the policy, and then 2000 hit followed by 2001 and 2002. The market was down for three straight years, causing my policy to lose money at an alarming rate. At this point I had two options, I could either double my premium payments to keep the policy afloat, which I did not have the money to do, or I could let the policy lapse because there was no longer enough money in the policy to cover the insurance costs. I let the policy lapse and lost all my money.

I do not want this to happen to you, which is why I am such a fan of indexed universal life insurance. A good indexed policy will provide a reasonable rate of return (5 to 7%), and will include a floor where, if the market drops, you do not lose any of your principal. This is why indexed universal life insurance policies are considered a good principal protected product.

Low fees: You will be hard-pressed to find very many books, or advisors for that matter, that mention low fees and life insurance in the same sentence. But if correctly structured, your life insurance policy can be a low-fee investment. What is considered a low-fee investment? An investment where the fees are no more than what a traditional money manager would charge. The current range for these fees is between 1 to 1.5%.

There is a big difference though in how a life insurance company charges fees and how a money manager charges fees, and this is where many people start to believe permanent insurance is a bad deal. Money managers usually charge an annual fee that is a percentage of your investable assets. Let us look at an example to see how this works.

Example: Cody has $100,000 he wants to invest and has contacted a local money manager by the name of Alisha to help him out. After reviewing Cody's risk tolerance and goals, Alisha offers Cody a contract to manage his investments for a 1.5% fee. Cody agrees to work with Alisha and transfers his assets and pays her $1,500 for her services. The next year rolls around and Cody's $100,000 is now $110,000. His new fee to Alisha is $1,650. This payment will go up and down each year based on the performance of Cody's investment portfolio.

A life insurance company on the other hand, will charge you an upfront fee that may be as high as 15%. From what I have told you so far, you can see why people consider permanent insurance expensive and why it only seems logical for someone like Cody to put all his investments with Alisha. But what people forget is the insurance company is including something with these higher upfront fees that Alisha cannot offer – permanent life insurance. The benefit of the life insurance is the magic that can make permanent life insurance policy a low fee investment.

Let us look at another example to see how this works.

Example: Joshua has $100,000 he wants to invest into an indexed universal life insurance policy. He meets Kayden, who is a local agent. Kayden runs an illustration for Joshua. This illustration includes, among other things, the annual cost of the policy. The initial fee, including the cost of insurance, is $15,000. But in return, Joshua gets a death benefit of $1,000,000. The illustration also shows that the longer Joshua owns the policy, the lower the fees, including the cost of insurance, go. Finally, getting down to .15% in its final years.

As you take this additional information into consideration you start to realize your additional $13,500 investment in the first year comes with an amazing rate of return if you happen to pass away earlier than expected. But what happens if you don't pass away? Do the higher upfront fees still make sense? They do if you treat your policy as a good marriage – you keep it until death do you part. If you have ever been married or been involved in a marriage, you know there are a lot of upfront costs. These costs include the ring, the wedding, the honeymoon, and maybe even a new house or new car. For those of you who are like me and have been married for years, you realized this upfront investment was well worth it over time. But if you got divorced shortly after the wedding, you probably did not consider your marriage a particularly worthwhile investment. You spent a bunch of money on all this stuff with nothing to show for it.

Permanent life insurance works the same way. If you are looking to buy the policy for the short term, please do yourself a favor and do not buy it. You will lose money, unless you happen to die unexpectedly before you can cancel the policy. But if you can hold onto the policy until "death do you part", you will find the fees, including the cost of insurance, will average out to be between 1 and 1.5%.

Because the cost of insurance plays such a big part in the fees associated with a permanent life insurance policy, most policies will only qualify as low fee policies if you are under age 70 when you purchase the policy and in reasonably good health.

Tax-free and cost-free distributions: Keeping the policy tax-free is easy. Just make sure you follow the contribution guidelines included in your policy, so it does not turn into a modified endowment contract (MEC). And have one dollar left in the cash value of the policy when you pass away as explained earlier in this chapter. If you do these two things, your investment growth inside of the policy and your distributions will all be tax-free. The cost-free side is the tricky part. Many top-tier insurance companies will charge you as much as 4% per year on any money you take out of the policy while you are alive. If this happens, which it easily could since one of the main reasons people have permanent insurance in retirement is so they can have tax-free income, you will lose tens of thousands of dollars to your insurance carrier. This is money that if you were with the right insurance company you would never have had to pay. If you are planning to take any money out of your policy while you are alive, you want to make sure your policy offers cost-free distributions.

Cost-free Chronic Illness Rider: This free rider is one of the key benefits that make permanent life insurance so special. I discussed how this rider works back in Chapter 8, but for those who are skipping around through the book I will go over it again. This rider allows you to access a portion of your death benefit prior to death if you have a long-term care event. All you must do to access the death benefit early is to get a doctor to sign off confirming you cannot do two out of the six activities of daily living. As explained earlier in the book, most policies will allow you to access about 24% of the death benefit per year for up to four years for a long-term care event. This benefit is then adjusted down to your age at the time of your first distribution as a percent of 100. The insurance company will hold about 1% of your death benefit back each year to use to keep the policy in force in case you end up using the benefits for the full four years.

Example: Jackie is 88 years old, and her physician just confirmed she cannot do two of the six activities of daily living and is now permanently disabled. This makes her eligible to exercise the no-fee chronic illness rider on her life insurance policy. The total death benefit on her policy is $400,000. In year one, she will be eligible for 24% of her death benefit reduced to 88%, or $84,480. Let's assume she is still in the facility in year two; she will be eligible for an additional $84,480. In year three, Jackie passes away. Her beneficiaries will receive the remaining 52% of her death benefit.

The right indexed universal life insurance policy is going to offer all the benefits I have discussed in this chapter, which is why I have implemented two of these policies into my retirement as well.

PRO TIP

Use principal protected products like indexed annuities and life insurance to maximize your retirement.

CHAPTER FOURTEEN

FIVE STRATEGIES TO A RISK-FREE RETIREMENT

You are now familiar with the risks and some of the products you can use to help eliminate these risks. It is time for you to learn what you need to do to get safely through retirement. In this chapter, you will learn five strategies you can use to increase your chances of having your money last as long as you do.

STRATEGY #1 - TAKE TIME TO UNDERSTAND SOCIAL SECURITY & MEDICARE

As you learned earlier in Chapters 3 and 10, Social Security and Medicare are both overly complex programs that require your attention if you want the best chance of getting your maximum benefits. Each year people experience major financial consequences because they make the wrong choice as it relates to their available benefits from these two programs.

You will want to start looking into your available Social Security benefits earlier than your Medicare benefits because your benefits become available sooner and they offer more flexibility. Analyzing your Social Security benefits by age 60 will provide you with the time you need to figure out the best claiming strategy for your situation. While doing your research, there are several things you need to consider. At what age should I apply for Social Security to maximize my benefits? How will the age I apply for Social Security affect my family members? How will additional years of earnings affect my benefits? Can I retire and wait to claim my Social Security benefits until a later date?

All of these are important considerations and can have a significant impact on your future benefits as you can see in the following example.

Example: After graduating from college at the age of 25 with her accounting degree, Jasmyn started her own accounting firm. Her firm was an immediate success, and her income has been above the Social Security threshold throughout her career. She is now 60 and would like to stop working and spend more time on her investments, but she is afraid her Social Security will be negatively affected. Based on Jasmyn's facts, she will see minimal impact on her benefits because she already has 35 years of high earnings. Therefore, any additional earnings will create minimal increases in her benefits.

As explained earlier, your initial enrollment period for Medicare lasts seven months. It starts on the first day of the month three months prior to your 65th birth month and ends on the last day of the month three months after your 65th birth month. Not everyone is going to need to sign up for Medicare during this initial enrollment period, but if you do you will need to know what the best way is for you to sign up for Medicare. The best way you can prepare yourself is to get an early start, which is why I suggest you start looking at Medicare at age 64.

Establish an account with the Social Security Administration - This should only take you between 10 and 15 minutes, so I suggest you do this today if you haven't already done so. You can establish an online Social Security account by going to www.ssa.gov. Once you have an account set up with the Social Security Administration, you get access to a lot of information that will help you better plan for your retirement. The most important information you will get access to is your Social Security benefit statement. This statement is going to provide you with a wealth of information on the Social Security benefits you are entitled to and how those benefits will change based on the age you decide to claim your benefits. Since Social Security is the foundation of a secure retirement, your retirement plan will not be complete without including your Social Security benefits as part of your plan.

Educate yourself on the pros and cons of both programs - It is one thing to have someone else tell you how Social Security and Medicare work; it is quite another to understand how these programs work yourself. Now, I am not telling you to become an expert in both programs, but I do recommend you understand the laws as they relate to your facts and circumstances. Your best option is to always confirm the law behind any strategy you have been advised to take as it relates to either of these programs. You may be able to confirm your knowledge through various website searches, but I have found both www.ssa.gov and www.medicare.gov to be very helpful in getting a better understanding of applicable law.

Meet with an advisor or broker to confirm your understanding of both programs - I realize you might be one who prefers to take your retirement into your own hands, but when it comes to retirement choices, it usually is not what you know but what you do not know that gets you into trouble. Advisors or brokers can provide immense value in helping you make better decisions on Social Security and Medicare. They can also be a great resource when dealing with claims or other problems you might have because of either program.

Do not rely on the government to help you out - There are things the government does well such as helping you process the necessary paperwork you must file to receive Social Security and Medicare benefits, helping you better understand the benefits you are receiving, and answering simple questions. But there are other things they do not do so well with. One of them is answering complex questions on Social Security and Medicare. If you are planning to contact either agency to get questions answered about their program, I suggest you reach out multiple times. I have found that many people get different answers each time they reach out, even though they are asking the same question. It is critical for your financial future that you get the correct answers to Social Security and Medicare and you understand the benefits and consequences of your decisions.

I have had problems with this twice within the last year just within my own family. The first experience happened with my sister. She and her husband were living in Arizona with their 15 year old son when her husband passed away due to COVID. Since he was already retired, all three of them were receiving Social Security benefits off his work record at the time of his death. My sister knew she was still entitled to Social Security benefits for her and her son even though her husband had died, but she didn't know how much she was entitled to. She called Social Security to let them know her husband had passed and to find out what the new benefit amounts were for her and her son. The agent on the phone gave her an amount. She then called me to tell me what he had told her she was entitled to. The amount the agent told her was wrong. I gave her the correct amount and she called back to get an agent who could help her get the correct benefits she was entitled to. She again got a different amount. It was not until her third time calling and after having received one payment that was for the wrong amount that they finally got it right.

The second time was with my adopted daughter, Alexis. Alexis came to my family from the Tennessee foster care system. She had been in and out of various homes and hospitals through-out her life and had various caretakers, including her biological mom and grandma. Knowing this, we decided to apply for a new Social Security number once we had her name changed after the adoption. To take care of this, my wife, Lisa, went down to our local Social Security office. As she sat down across from the em-ployee she would be working with, she was asked what she was there to have done. Lisa informed the person on the other side of the desk that she was there to get a new Social Security number for Alexis, who we had just adopted. She was shocked when the employee told her that was impossible, since adoption was not a qualifying reason to get a new number. Knowing better, Lisa told the employee she would wait while he went back and talked to his manager about what needed to be done to make this happen. The employee returned after about five minutes. As he sat down to his computer, he said, "I am sorry. You are right, Mrs. Hall. You can get a new Social Security number for your daughter. All I must do is click this box that says she has been adopted and click this box stating you want a new number. I will be back with the new card shortly." Had my wife not known the laws governing Social Security better than their own employee, she would have left the office empty handed that day.

STRATEGY #2 - USE A THREE BUCKET SYSTEM

There are millions of different options out there you can use to plan for your retirement. But if you are looking to get to a risk-free retirement there is no reason to make it over complicated. The foundation for a risk-free retirement starts with a base of Social Security and then an allocation of all other retirement assets and income into three different buckets.

Taxable Bucket	Tax-Deferred Bucket	Tax-Free Bucket
Cash Accounts	Individual Retirement Account (IRA)	Roth IRA
Certificates of Deposit	401(k)/403(b)/457	Roth 401(k)
Stock/Bonds	Self-Employed Pension (SEP)	Roth SEP
Real Estate	SIMPLE Plan	Permanent Life Insurance

Taxable bucket – This bucket is designed to be used in case of emergencies, which means the assets in this bucket should be liquid. Surprisingly, the amount of money you should have in this bucket is something most advisors agree on. You should have six months of basic living expenses in this bucket when you hit retirement. Anything over six months of basic living expenses will subject these assets to unnecessary risk, and anything less than six months of basic living expenses may put you at risk of an emergency disrupting your other retirement assets. I usually recommend that assets in this bucket be invested in savings accounts or money market accounts, since the money in this bucket is designed for safety not performance.

Tax-deferred bucket – Of those who have saved for retirement, many of you have overfunded this bucket. There is a mathematically correct balance you should have in this bucket. Your amount will be different from anyone else. Since I cannot calculate your amount in this book, let me provide you with the guidelines you should use to get this bucket funded properly. First, you want assets that are low enough in value that your required minimum distributions (RMDs) will be low enough not to exceed your standard deduction. If you do this, you get a double win. You did not pay tax on the money going into the tax-deferred bucket, and you will not be paying tax on the money once you start your RMDs either. Second, you want your RMDs to be low enough they do not create provisional income and cause your Social Security to be taxed. If you can get your tax-deferred accounts down low enough to meet these two criteria, most of you can get to a tax-free retirement.

If you are single, the maximum amount you should have in the tax-deferred bucket is $250,000. If you are married, the maximum amount you should have in the tax-deferred bucket is $500,000. The lower your Social Security income is and the less taxable income you have, the more money you will be able to put in this bucket. If you have high taxable income from things like pensions or rental income, you may need your tax-deferred bucket to be zero to limit future tax exposure. Many of you will need to do Roth conversions to get this bucket where it needs to be.

Tax-free bucket – Once you have the right amount in your taxable and tax-deferred buckets, you want to put everything else in your tax-free bucket. This is the one bucket you can never put too much money in because assets in this bucket are structured to be tax-free for as long as you live.

STRATEGY #3 - START FILLING YOUR TAX-FREE BUCKET

Most people think they should wait until they retire to start contributing to their tax-free bucket because they have come to believe their taxes will be lower during their retirement years. As I explained earlier in the book, what I have found is this is not true for many people because of lost deductions, provisional income, and a government that is spending money unlike anything I have ever seen. As a result, many people will be facing a much higher tax rate in retirement than they are today. Some of the things you can do are implementing Roth conversions, redirecting your retirement contributions to Roth accounts, putting a Roth annuity in place, and looking into buying an indexed universal life insurance policy.

STRATEGY #4 - USE PRINCIPAL PROTECTED PRODUCTS

A good rule of thumb for how much of your portfolio should be principal protected is to take your age as a percent of 100. This means if you are 60 years old and have retirement assets of $1,000,000, you should have about $600,000 of these assets protected to where if the market were to go down, you would not lose any money. As mentioned earlier, the two principal protected products I like are fixed indexed annuities and an indexed universal life policy. Principal protected products do not include money market accounts, CDs, or any other product insured by FDIC because these assets have historically not made large enough returns to keep up with inflation.

STRATEGY #5 - CREATE A RISK-BASED RETIREMENT PLAN

Everything you have learned in this book or have already done up to this point for your retirement has little value if you do not move forward and create a risk-based retirement plan. If structured correctly, a risk-based plan will not only tell you if you will have enough income to last through your retirement, but it will also tell you whether you will have any assets left to pass on to beneficiaries. Also, please remember, the purpose of this plan is not to show the best possible outcome for your retirement. The purpose of the plan is to figure out if you can make it financially through retirement if your retirement ends up being subject to any, or all, of the risks I have gone over in this book.

On Christmas Day in 2015, Lisa, myself, five of our six children, two dogs, fourteen suitcases, and seven carry-ons moved to Puerto Rico. Knowing the island could have a hurricane at any time, I decided I needed to prepare for the worst but hope for the best. It was probably the Eagle Scout coming out in me, or maybe just the fact my parents and my church drilled preparedness into me since I was a kid. Regardless, there were many things I put in place to protect my family in case a hurricane did hit the island. I bought a concrete home. I did this because it is my belief a home is not of much value if it ever gets moved from where it was originally built. I had thousands of dollars of cash in my home because

I knew if there was ever a problem with electricity or the banking system, this money would help me buy the goods and services I needed until these systems could be restored. I loaded my garage with food and water because I knew if a hurricane hit, these two items may be hard to find. Then I waited – prepared for the worst, but still hoped for the best.

On September 20, 2017, hurricane Maria hit the island with winds of more than 100 miles per hour. Over the course of a few hours, Maria destroyed the island and many of the lives of those who lived there. But because of what we had done to prepare when there was no storm in sight, our family was not one of them, even though we were without water for three weeks and power for 50 days. Our home was not damaged during the storm. I never had to stand in line at the bank hoping to be able to draw money out of my account. I very seldom had to wait in the long food or water lines that formed on the island. Instead, I served and spent time together with my loved ones. Because of our preparedness, we were also able to house a family of four from Tortola whose daughter had been medically evacuated. Yes, it was hard, and I hope it is something I never have to go through again, but we survived.

Why am I telling you this story? Because your risk-based plan is going to be designed to provide you with the same comfort my preparedness provided me when I was in the eye of a hurricane. You will hope you never experience the risks I have covered in this book, but if you do, you will be prepared.

Here is a list of things you need to include when creating your risk-based retirement plan.

Double future tax rates – David Walker arguably knows more about the economy and the future of taxes than anyone in the country, and this doubling of taxes is what he has projected needs to happen. It may take us a while to get there, but this could easily become our new reality around 2030.

Show a reasonable rate of return (4.0-5.0%) - Remember, the purpose of this plan is not to show home runs on your investment account. A reasonable rate of return for most retirees has proven to be right between 4 and 5% after fees.

Inflation adjusts your annual income – You might be sleeping through part of your retirement, but inflation will not be. If you look back over time, you will find the average inflation rate in America has been just under 3%, which is the inflation percentage I currently use in most of my planning.

Maximize your Social Security benefits – There is nothing illegal or immoral about getting every dollar from the Social Security program that is rightfully yours, but you should not expect the government to help you do this. You may need to hire a professional to help you make sure you are applying for your benefits at the optimal time based on your facts and circumstances.

Plan for a long-term care event – Self-insure, rely on a family member, buy a long-term care policy, or a life insurance policy with a chronic illness rider. These are your options, and I am not here to tell you which one is the right one, but I am here to tell you to choose at least one of them. With a 35% chance of becoming permanently disabled, you need to have a solution for a long-term care event.

Principal protect a portion of assets – Take your age and divide it into 100%. As mentioned earlier this is the percentage of your retirement assets you should have invested into principal protected assets like indexed annuities or indexed universal life policies. This means that if you are 60, you should have 60% of your assets principal protected. If you are 70, you should have 70% protected.

Calculate an appropriate withdrawal rate – For many of you, this is going to be as low as 2.5-3.0%, but with the right planning, you should be able to increase this percentage to as high as 6 or 7%.

Project lifetime income to age one hundred – Average life expectancy has not reached 100, but it does not mean you will not still be alive when you turn 100. When putting together a risk-based plan, it is far better to overestimate life expectancy than to underestimate it.

Budget for increased medical costs – With increased life expectancy and increases in medical costs, your cost of healthcare in retirement may be much higher than you expect. You need to make sure you have something to cover these potential costs.

Create multiple streams of tax-free income – A retirement filled with tax-deferred income and Social Security will not provide you with the security you need for your retirement. Your safest way to plan for your future retirement is to have multiple streams of tax-free income.

Remember any plan is just a plan. It is not intended to be a guarantee of what will happen in the future. Plans are created to give you the best chance of having the positive outcomes the plan proposes.

CHAPTER FIFTEEN

WHAT DO I NEED TO DO NEXT?

You may be feeling a little overwhelmed right now, and it is okay. You are not alone. At this point, I have educated over 175,000 CPAs on the concepts you have just read about and many of them are overwhelmed too. The good news is, it is not too late to act. You now know what the Top 10 Financial Risks Facing Your Retirement are. You have 5 strategies to help you reduce or eliminate each of these risks. You also have me, which is far more than most Americans have. Your next step is to start implementing what you have learned into your own retirement plan. To do this, you have two options.

The first option is to take the hard road and create your own risk-based retirement plan. If you have the time, the software, a resource for principal protected products, and the knowledge you need to do this, you will find the process of creating a plan enlightening. The second option is to allow my team and me to help you. We already have the expensive proprietary software needed to create your risk-based plan, we have decades of experience in what it takes to eliminate the risks facing your retirement, and we have access to the products that have the bells and whistles you will need to succeed.

If you decide to move forward with my team the process will look like this:

- We will start by getting to know you and gathering all the information we need to analyze your current retirement situation. We will find out what you want to do with your money while you are alive and what you want to happen to your money once you die.

- We will then create a traditional retirement plan. This plan will look like the traditional retirement plans other advisors are providing for their clients. It will start with all the information you provided us with regarding your retirement. It will then take into consideration average rates of return, historical inflation rates, and how much you want to distribute each year. The result will be a plan that shows you how long your retirement income and assets are expected to last by using these limited assumptions.

- The next thing we will do is create a second plan. This second plan will take your retirement assets as they currently sit, but it is going to be put under the stress of the risks I have covered in this book. What if taxes double? What impact is inflation going to have? What happens if you live beyond life expectancy? What if you have a long-term care event? What if you claim your Social Security at the wrong time? This plan is designed to help you better understand the impact each of these risks can have on your retirement.

- We will then create a third plan, which we call the risk-based retirement plan. The purpose of this third plan is to provide you with the solutions you need to reduce or eliminate the various risks facing your retirement. This third plan will be the one you use for your future retirement and will come with a roadmap that has step-by-step instructions on what you need to do to optimize your retirement.
- Once your risk-based retirement plan is created ,our certified team of advisors will sit down with you and review it. We will explain each step in the roadmap. We will review the insurance and annuity illustrations, if there are any. And finally, we will spend the necessary time answering any and all questions you may have regarding this plan.
- Our next task is to work with you as a partner to implement any strategies, to make any required adjustments to the initial plan so you have a final product, and to be there along the way to adjust and update the plan as needed.

DO NOT WAIT UNTIL IT IS TOO LATE

I had most of my risk-based retirement plan put together by the time I was 48 and I am sure glad I took care of it early. As mentioned earlier in the book, I moved to Puerto Rico in 2015. While there, I went in for a check-up with my doctor only to find out I had kidney failure and was going to need a transplant. I knew this could be a possibility because my grandmother had died of kidney failure, my mom had died of kidney failure, I had a sister who had already had a transplant, and a brother who was on dialysis.

During the time Lisa and I were trying to figure out how we were going to manage this, Lisa ended up at lunch one day with a friend she had met on the island, named Jen. Lisa explained to her our situation, and they spent the rest of their time together discussing the impact this would have on our family. A little while later, Lisa and Jen got back together and part of what they talked about was my kidney failure and what it would take to find a donor. Lisa didn't know everything but explained that the first requirement is the donor must have the same blood type. Not much more was said about this until they were both getting ready to leave, and Jen asked, "What is Dave's blood type?" Lisa responded, "It is 0+." Lisa left not giving Jen's final question a second thought.

A week or so later they got back together for lunch again when Jen informed Lisa that she was going to donate me her kidney. Lisa was shocked and quickly turned the discussion to another topic, believing this was not something she could ask Jen to do. They left lunch that day and Lisa came home and told me what Jen said. As much as we were happy at what she was offering, we both came to the realization this was not something we could ask her to do, so we dropped the topic.

Another week or two went by ,and Lisa and Jen went to lunch again. During this lunch, Jen was the first to bring up the topic of my kidney problems by asking Lisa, "Why did you never respond when I told you I was going to give your husband my kidney?" Lisa did not really know what to say because she was embarrassed but finally got up the courage to tell Jen we couldn't ask her to do this. Jen responded, "You are not asking me to do this. I am telling you I am going to do this."

To make a long story short, I had Jen's kidney transplanted in me on October 30, 2019, in Auxilio Mutuo Hospital in Puerto Rico.

Her kidney ended up being a better match than if I had been able to get a kidney from one of my siblings. I will forever be indebted to Jen and her family for such a selfless gift.

As touching as this story is, it also helps to prove another very important point about your retirement planning. You do not want to put it off any longer because something could happen in your life that makes it impossible to take all the steps needed to get to a risk-free retirement. I put most of my risk-based retirement plan together years ago, and I am so grateful I did because there would be no way I could get "low fee" insurance at this point in my life.

IT SHOULD BE FORO NOT FOMO

A current slang term that has taken the country by storm is what the younger generation calls FOMO – the fear of missing out. It may make sense during our younger days, but I wish I could remove this concept from the minds of those planning for their retirement. It is causing individuals to make bad decisions they shouldn't be making. Let me walk you through a few examples that I have experienced with actual clients in hopes of helping it make more sense. All names have been changed to protect the guilty.

Example: Chris and Courtney get to the part in our planning where I review with them my recommendation on when they should claim their Social Security benefits. From my analysis, I conclude that Courtney should wait until age 70 to claim her benefits and Chris should claim his benefits at 66. I then explained to them why I recommend these ages, how longevity plays into the calculation, and how their plan will allow them to have the money the need each year even if they wait.

Once I finished, I asked, "Do you have any questions or concerns?" Courtney was the first to speak, "Yes, I have major concerns with what you are proposing. You are showing breakeven under this scenario at 81 years old. I have never had anyone in my family live to that age. I am not waiting. If I die early like my family has, I am going to miss out on tens of thousands of dollars in money I am owed from the government." Chris nodded his head in agreement.

"I understand your concern Courtney, and please know you are not alone in your thinking. Over 25% of those I work with have this similar concern," I stated, before asking, "Does this mean you are willing to risk running out of money just because you have an axe to grind with the government?"

Chris jumped into the conversation, "What do you mean? Can you explain what you are talking about?"

"Yes, I can, and I will. If you remember from our last meeting when we reviewed your three plans, all three plans showed you could take out the $100,000 you had projected to cover your lifestyle each year past age 81. Therefore, I see absolutely no upside to what you are recommending. If you move forward with your plan and live longer than you expect, you could easily end up having a Social Security only retirement. But if you are patient and wait to claim using the maximum strategy, what is the worst thing that will happen?" I paused for a few seconds to see if they would answer, but they did not, so I proceeded to answer the question myself. "The worst thing that will happen to you is you will have the exact same retirement you would have had if you claimed your Social Security at age 62 because both plans are designed to give you the same amount of income up until your breakeven age."

It was Courtney's turn again. "Okay. I can see what you are saying, but what about my kids? They will inherit less if we follow your plan and end up dying young because we will have used more of their inheritance during the initial spend down period."

I responded, "Good point, but let me ask you another question. In my scenario, you risk missing out on some Social Security and leaving a smaller inheritance if you die young. In your scenario you risk running out of money and dying broke. Which problem do you think your kids would rather have to deal with - the risk of having a smaller inheritance or the risk of having to pay your bills because you ran out of money?"

"I don't think our kids could afford to take care of us and their own families," Chris quipped.

This example really brings out a couple of things. First, far too many of us have a fear of missing out. Second, too many of us are still trying to put the mask on the kids first. Third, we continue to underestimate our life expectancy. The other thing you should note is that I have worked with thousands of clients throughout my career, and I have never had one of their kids come back after they died and complain that their parents could have had a larger inheritance if they made a different decision with their Social Security. It just doesn't happen, folks.

Example: AnnaLee and Bud got to the part in our planning where I was reviewing tax rate risk. I was going through the proposed Roth conversions. Their plan showed they needed to convert $100,000 for the next 5 years at an annual tax cost of just under $25,000. Once I was finished, I asked, "Do you have any questions or concerns?" With a puzzled look on his face, Bud spoke up, "Yes, I do. I am having a hard time wrapping my head around the fact that taxes could double. I have spent my whole life trying to defer the taxes on my retirement assets so I would only have to pay a portion of the tax each year for the rest of my life. This goes against everything I believe, and I cannot do this."

After Bud finished, I stated, "I understand this is new information and that it goes against everything you have been taught, but let me ask you a few questions. Do you believe taxes will ever be lower than they are today with all the unfunded liabilities you learned about in my webinar?" "No, I don't think so," Bud replies. "Based upon what I showed you about your own tax rates and taxation of your Social Security in our last meeting, do you see a day in the future where you will be paying taxes at a lower rate than you are today?" I asked. "No," Bud once again answered.

Here is my last question, "Do you believe if taxes do go up by 2030, as your plan projects, that doing a Roth conversion now would be a good idea?" Both Bud and AnnaLee nodded their heads yes. "Then let's look at the benefits and consequences of either decision. If you are right and taxes do not go up, but they also don't go down, what will happen? The exact same tax will be paid on your tax-deferred assets as you would pay today. Plus, you will always be worrying in the back of your mind whether you made the right decision. But what if I am right? What if taxes do double at some time in your retirement? You will have gotten a huge win. You not only won't have to pay the higher taxes, but you won't have to worry if the tax man could ruin your retirement. The other thing you must take into consideration if you don't pay the taxes now is what are your kids' tax rates? Due to the way they are taxed, tax-deferred assets are the worst assets you can transfer to your children."

What do we learn from this example? First, people are still concerned about missing out. Second, we often fail to think through our planning and how it might impact our children. Third, old beliefs are hard to overcome.

In the end, what is the biggest concern in each of these examples? Both couples have a fear of missing out. Chris and Courtney are afraid they will miss out on extra Social Security benefits and AnnaLee and Bud are afraid they will miss out on some future tax benefits. Folks, it is time you change the way you think about retirement. Instead of the fear of missing out, you need to change to the fear of running out (FORO). A risk-based plan was not designed by Dave Ramsey, where to make it to the end of your retirement with the lifestyle you want you are going to have to eat rice and beans in your early years of retirement. A risk-based plan is designed to give you the lifestyle you want throughout your retirement without the fear of running out. In fact, the crazy thing about a risk-based plan is the longer you live the better it gets. This is completely opposite of most traditional plans.

PUT YOUR MASK ON FIRST

If you have ever flown on an airplane, you probably remember sitting through a safety briefing by the flight attendant before takeoff. In this presentation the flight attendant tells you that if the cabin loses pressure oxygen masks will drop from the ceiling. Once these masks drop, you are to put your mask on first, and then help put a mask on any young children you might be traveling with. Why do they suggest you handle the masks in this order? Because if you don't take care of yourself first, you may not live long enough to take care of those you love.

There are two principles in this example that apply to your retirement. First, if you go about trying to take care of others' financial needs before you take care of your own retirement needs, you risk not having enough money to cover your retirement. Second, if you take care of your needs first, chances are there will be something left you can pass on to those you love.

I do not know who you have in your life you are hoping to leave a legacy to, but I have a couple of kids depending on me, and I do not want to let them down. I mentioned at the first of the book that my wife, Lisa, and I have eight children. But the part of the story I left out is that two of these children have severe disabilities where they will never be able to take care of themselves. We found both Alexis and Kayden through the Tennessee foster care system where they both experienced some level of abuse and neglect. If there is anything I can do about it, I will never let them go back into a system where they can be taken advantage of again. Which means I must have a plan, since both of their life expectancies are longer than mine.

Research has been done that shows 96% of financial advisors do not invest in the products they recommend for their clients, but I am not one of them. I am part of the 4%. Everything I have talked about in this book I have done for my own retirement. I have created a plan that is designed to help me achieve my goals. I own indexed life insurance. I own three annuities. I have a long-term care policy I paid for up front. I know when I am supposed to take my Social Security to maximize my benefits. In short, I have a plan that will allow me to live the same lifestyle I currently live during my retirement years, no matter how long they happen to be. And I can leave millions of dollars to my two disabled children, so they can continue to live the life they have now become accustomed to.

What are you waiting for? Today is your day to act. Today is your day to prepare for a retirement that will not always be smooth and easy. Today is your day to show those you love you are doing what it takes to achieve success. A risk-free retirement is not going to happen by itself. It needs effort, and my team and I are here to help you achieve your goals and dreams. You can find us at www.retirementriskadvisors.com. I look forward to hearing from you soon.

CASE STUDY CARLOS AND MARIA GARCIA

To help you better understand the impact that the risks I have covered in this book can have on your retirement, I am providing this case study. Remember, this is a case study and not your retirement plan. Your facts and circumstances will be different than Carlos and Maria Garcia's (names changed), but the risks are still the same. Use this case study to help you better identify the holes you have in your own retirement.

STEP 1 – GET TO KNOW THE GARCIAS AND GATHER THEIR FINANCIAL INFORMATION

Carlos & Maria Garcia are both retired. Carlos is age 66 and Maria is age 62. Mrs. Garcia spent most of her life in the home taking care of her two children, so spousal benefits from Social Security will provide Mrs. Garcia with a higher Social Security benefit than her own work record. They are planning to apply for Social

Security benefits now, since Carlos is finally retired. The Garcias' pre-retirement income was $120,000 and they are planning to spend $90,000 in after-tax money each year in retirement. They have no permanent life insurance, long-term care insurance, or annuities. They have done a pretty good job of saving and have the following assets for their retirement:

THE GARCIAS' ASSETS

- Taxable bucket - $500,000 (local bank/CDs)
- Tax-deferred bucket - $1,500,000 (Carlos's IRA)
- Tax-free bucket - $0

Their combined Social Security, assuming a full retirement age of 66 for Mr. Garcia and Mrs. Garcia starting to claim her benefits at age 62, is $33,750.

THEIR GOALS

The Garcias want to make sure they are taking care of themselves first, so their goal is to be able to maintain the same lifestyle in retirement they enjoyed during their working years. Once they pass away, they are hoping to leave as much money as possible for their two children. They both already have young families and are experiencing the financial stresses family life creates.

STEP 2 - CREATE A TRADITIONAL RETIREMENT PLAN

I currently use a 3% inflation rate for all my plans. Inflation rates over the last 100 years have averaged 2.8%. I will also use a 5% average rate of return. There are times I may lower this down, but I usually don't have to. Then I will add these assumptions with the information I received from the Garcias to create a traditional plan. Here is how theirs turned out.

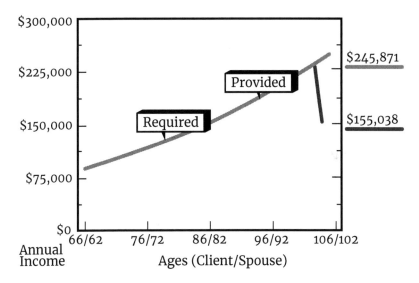

What are the results of the traditional plan? It looks amazing. They are not expected to run out of money until Carlos turns 100 and it shows they will have a high probability of having money left over for their two kids. Unfortunately, the Garcias' traditional plan has a problem. Their plan is still subject to every risk I have covered in this book, which is why we need to create additional plans.

STEP 3 – ANALYZE EACH RISK AND CRE-ATE A STRESS TESTED PLAN

To get started with this step, we need to analyze each of the ten risks and see what impact they may have on their retirement.

RISK # 1 (A)
SOCIAL SECURITY RISK
Taking Benefits at the Wrong Age

Carlos's FRA Benefit	$25,000
Maria's Age 62 Benefit	<u>$ 8,750</u>
Total Benefit	**$33,750**
Carlos's Age 70 Benefit	$33,000
Maria's FRA Benefit	<u>$ 12,500</u>
Total Benefit	**$45,500**

The extra Social Security benefits the Garcias will receive by the ages of 70 and 66 if they are to claim their benefits at 66 and 62 is $135,000. This is a lot of money, but it can start disappearing extremely fast when we start looking at longevity. If they are willing to wait until 70 and 66 to claim their Social Security benefits, their annual benefit will increase by $11,750 over what they would receive by claiming at 66 and 62.

In the Garcias situation, breakeven is 11.5 years at Carlos's age 81.5 and Maria's age 77.5. At these ages it will not matter whether the Garcias claimed early or late, they will have received the same amount of money in Social Security benefits. But at these two ages they haven't even made it to life expectancy yet. Assuming the Garcias live to the average life expectancy of 84 for a male and 88 for a female, they will get an additional $93,375 in benefits. You may be asking, "If these numbers are so good, why doesn't Maria just wait until age 70 too?" If you remember from earlier in the book, it is because there are no delayed retirement credits for spousal benefits, which is the benefit that will provide her with the most income from Social Security.

As you can see from the above calculation, if the Garcias decide to move forward claiming Social Security at age 66 and 62, they will end up leaving tens of thousands of dollars on the table with the Social Security administration if they even live to life expectancy.

RISK #1 (B)
SOCIAL SECURITY RISK
Taxability of Benefits

	No SS Taxation	With SS Taxation
Annual IRA income ($1,500,000 x4.5%)	$67,500	$67,500
Social Security income ($33,750 x 85%)	_____	$28,687
Total taxable income	$67,500	$96,187
Less the standard deduction	($27,300)	($27,300)
Taxable income	$40,200	$68,887
Federal tax	$4,413	$7,855

Additional tax due to Social Security being taxed $3,442 per year (78% increase)

Wow. This additional tax will cause the Garcias to spend more money each year than they otherwise would have had their Social Security not been subject to tax. This one error alone can cause them to run out of money 5 to 7 years faster than they otherwise would.

RISK #2
TAX RATE RISK
Taxes Higher in the Future

	Pre-Retirement Taxes	Retirement Taxes
Income	$110,000	$67,500
Social Security		$28,687
401(k) contribution	($20,500)	$0
Total taxable income	$89,500	$96,187
Less standard deduction	($25,900)	($27,300)
Taxable income	$63,600	$68,887
Federal Tax	$7,221	$ 7,855
Less child tax credit	($2,000)	
Less education credit	($2,500)	
Total tax owed	$2,751	$ 7,855

Additional taxes owed in retirement $5,134 (over 2.8 x more)

The Garcias' tax situation does not look much different than many of yours. They ended up losing their deductions in their retirement years, so although their gross income went down, their taxable income went up.

RISK #3
LONGEVITY RISK
Risk of Living Too Long

The longer Mr. and Mrs. Garcia live, the higher chance they will have issues with their retirement assets lasting as long as they do. The way traditional retirement plans are designed often leads to them looking worse the longer you live.

RISK #4
SEQUENCE OF RETURN RISK
Take Withdrawals in a Down Market

Year	Beginning Account Value	Projected Account Return	Distributions	Distributions Value
1	$1,500,000	- 9.00%*	$67,500	$1,297,500
2	$1,297,500	-11.89%*	$69,525	$1,073,702
3	$1,073,702	-22.10*	$71,610	$764,803

Withdrawal rate in the beginning – 4.5%

Withdrawal rate starting in Year 3 – 9.6%

Losses shown for each year are hypothetical and are using the S&P 500 losses for 2000, 2001, and 2002.

Unfortunately, Mr. and Mrs. Garcia are no different than any of you. They do not have a crystal ball to see what the stock market is going to do in the initial years after they retire. As a result, they could lose a sizable portion of their retirement assets during the first three years of their retirement if the market takes a downturn. This could cause them to run out of money 15 years faster than they otherwise would if they follow their traditional retirement plan.

RISK #5

WITHDRAWAL RATE RISK

Risk of Withdrawing Money Too Fast

All Observations		Annualized Withdrawal Rate of as % of initial Portfolio Value, Then Adjusted for CPI								
Final Asset Value Target = 0		3.00%	3.25%	3.50%	3.75%	4.00%	4.25%	4.50%	4.75%	5.00%
100% Stocks	30 Years	100%	100%	100%	99%	97%	94%	91%	86%	82%
	40 years	100%	100%	99%	97%	93%	88%	84%	80%	76%
	50 years	100%	100%	99%	95%	90%	85%	81%	77%	73%
	60 Years	100%	99%	98%	94%	89%	84%	80%	75%	70%
75% Stocks	30 Years	100%	100%	100%	100%	99%	95%	90%	84%	80%
	40 years	100%	100%	100%	98%	93%	86%	82%	76%	69%
	50 years	100%	100%	99%	94%	88%	82%	76%	69%	62%
	60 Years	100%	100%	97%	92%	85%	80%	71%	65%	58%
50% Stocks	30 Years	100%	100%	100%	100%	95%	91%	85%	77%	70%
	40 years	100%	100%	98%	93%	86%	76%	65%	59%	51%
	50 years	100%	98%	93%	85%	74%	63%	55%	46%	41%
	60 Years	100%	96%	89%	79%	65%	57%	48%	42%	36%
25% Stocks	30 Years	100%	100%	98%	90%	80%	70%	63%	57%	51%
	40 years	97%	89%	77%	64%	55%	47%	37%	34%	32%
	50 years	85%	75%	62%	51%	40%	34%	31%	29%	23%
	60 Years	78%	65%	51%	39%	33%	31%	27%	21%	17%
0% Stocks	30 Years	89%	80%	68%	61%	54%	50%	45%	40%	34%
	40 years	64%	56%	47%	39%	33%	29%	24%	21%	18%
	50 years	50%	39%	31%	27%	23%	19%	14%	12%	9%
	60 Years	35%	30%	25%	22%	16%	12%	9%	7%	7%

The initial distribution rate of 4.5% used by the Garcias was already too high if they are wanting the highest chance for their money to last them through retirement, but if they try to maintain their lifestyle after facing sequence of return risk, the new rate of 9.6% is going to be very problematic. By using the chart above you can see how fast specific rates would diminish the Garcias' funds (and even your own) faster than other rates.

LONG-TERM CARE RISK
Risk of Becoming Permanently Disabled

Estimated annual cost	$150,000
Projected # of years	3
Total estimated cost	$450,000
Total cash needed including tax	$492,000
Available assets prior to the event	
Taxable bucket	$500,000
Tax-deferred bucket	$764,803
Remaining assets after the event	
Taxable bucket	$260,000
Tax-deferred bucket	$512,803
Old withdrawal amounts	
Retirement assets	$73,758
Social Security	$33,750
New withdrawal amounts	
Retirement assets (4.5)	$23,481
Social security	$25,000

To show the impact of this risk, I am contemplating Carlos has a long-term care event first and chooses to live in a private facility. I am also assuming he dies after being in the facility for three years. Due to the annual cost charged by the facility to take care of Carlos, the Garcias would have spent down their assets much faster than anticipated had this long-term care event not happened. This spend down leaves Maria in a much worse financial position than she was prior to Carlos's death.

RISK #7

INFLATION RISK

Risk Inflation Will Erode Retirement Assets

Remaining cash in bank	$260,000
Projected inflation rate	3%
Projected buying power in 24 years	$130,000

The only inflation-adjusted income the Garcias have is Social Security. Therefore, Maria will be subject to inflation risk eating away at the buying power of her remaining assets throughout the rest of her retirement.

RISK #8

MEDICARE RISK

Risk of Claiming the Wrong Benefits at the Wrong Time

Mr. Garcia did not get any advice when signing up for Medicare. He was just looking for the cheapest option, so he signed up for a Medicare Advantage Plan. Mr. Garcia ended up being incredibly lucky, and the Medicare Advantage Plan he signed up for covers what he expected for his healthcare costs. Mrs. Garcia will not be able to sign up for Medicare until age 65.

RISK #9

ELDER ABUSE RISK

Risk of Financial Exploitation After Age 60

Due to their lack of planning, if the Garcias traditional retirement plan plays out like what has been modeled, Maria has a high chance of experiencing financial exploitation before she passes on. Not only has she lost her husband, who oversaw most of the financial decisions they needed to make, but she also does not have enough assets to live the lifestyle she has become accustomed to. Both situations put her at risk of being taken advantage of by someone who does not have her best interest in mind.

RISK #10

LACK OF INCOME DIVERSITY RISK

Risk of Not Having Enough Tax-Free Income Streams

With only taxable assets, tax-deferred assets, and Social Security, the Garcias do not have enough diversity in their retirement income to eliminate the risks facing their retirement.

Now that you have seen some of the things that can go wrong if you fail to remove the risks facing your retirement, it is time to start answering some questions for yourself. How much money could you potentially lose by claiming your Social Security benefits at the wrong time? What happens if taxes do double as David Walker says they must? How would living to age 100 impact your retirement? Could a market downturn during your early years of retirement cause you to run out of money 15 years earlier? Can you live off a 3% distribution rate, or would you rather have a plan in place to allow you to increase this amount? Can your retirement handle a 50% drop in buying power? What is your plan for Medicare? Are you okay with living in a Medicaid funded long-term care facility? As you can imagine, the list could go on and on, but I will stop here because hopefully you are getting the point.

STEP 4 – CREATE THE RISK-BASED RETIREMENT PLAN

Due to the complexity of what it takes to put a risk-based retirement plan together, I cannot walk you through all the details of what it took me to put the Garcias' risk-based retirement plan together in this book, but what I can show you is the results of the plan.

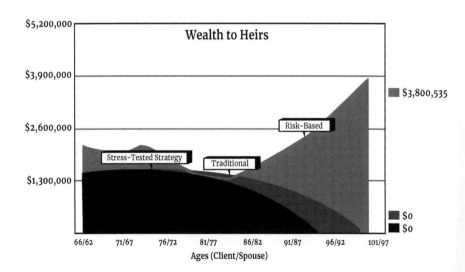

*For illustration purposes only. Actual results will differ from what is being projected.

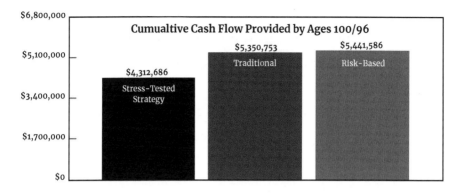

As you can see from the above images the risk-based retirement plan provides them a better chance to obtain their two main retirement goals. They are maintaining their same lifestyle and leaving as much money to their two kids as possible.

STEP 5 – EXPLAIN THE RISK-BASED RETIREMENT PLAN INCLUDING THE ROADMAP

With Mr. & Mrs. Garcia's risk-based retirement plan they also received a roadmap giving them step-by-step instructions on what they needed to do to complete the plan. Their plan included six steps. I will review each step along with the consequences and benefits.

1 - CLAIM SOCIAL SECURITY AT CARLOS'S AGE 70 AND MARIA'S AGE 66

- **Consequences** – None
- **Benefits** – The Garcias can increase the stability of a longer than expected retirement.
- **Main Risks Reduced or Eliminated** – Social Security Risk

2 - REVIEW CARLOS'S MEDICARE ADVANTAGE PLAN EACH YEAR AND SIGN MARIA UP AT AGE 65

- **Consequences** – None
- **Benefits** – The Garcias will be able to make sure they have the appropriate coverage for the medical costs they will incur during their retirement.
- **Main Risks Reduced or Eliminated** – Medicare Risk

3 - APPLY FOR PERMANENT LIFE INSURANCE FOR MR. & MRS. GARCIA

- **Consequences** – None
- **Benefits** – It will help the Garcias determine life expectancy. Estimated longevity is important too so we can have open discussions about any other potential changes we may need to make to the plan.
- **Main Risks Reduced or Eliminated** – Longevity Risk

4 - BUY TWO PERMANENT LIFE INSURANCE POLICIES

- **Consequences** – The amount invested will not be liquid for at least four years.
- **Benefits** – The Garcias can use the death benefit of the policies if they have a long-term care event. The amount invested in the insurance policy will grow tax-free, and they will be able to have the money distributed tax-free. The money they have invested is protected against loss if there is a downturn in the market. They have a death benefit they can transfer to their kids or a charity once they

pass away if the cash value has not been used for expenses during their lifetimes.

- **Main Risks Reduced or Eliminated** – Long-term care, tax-rate, and sequence of return risk

5 – USE PART OF THEIR TAX-DEFERRED ASSETS TO CONVERT INTO A ROTH ANNUITY

- **Consequences** – The Garcias will have to pay taxes on the money as they convert it to Roth. They will also lose some liquidity on the annuity versus the stock market.
- **Benefits** – The Garcias will be able to get a guaranteed, tax-free stream of income that will last as long as they do. By matching this income to their Social Security, the Garcias will have much less to worry about in retirement.
- **Main Risks Reduced or Eliminated** – Longevity, tax-rate, sequence of return, inflation, and withdrawal rate risk.

6 - COVER THEIR LIVING COSTS FOR 4 YEARS

- **Consequences** – The Garcias will be required to spend down assets to cover living expenses and will pay tax on the money they convert from their tax-deferred account.
- **Benefits** – The Garcias will be able to pay their taxes while we have historically low tax rates. They will be able to build income diversity. They will also be able to allow their other assets time to settle in, which will provide them with a more secure retirement.
- **Main Risks Reduced or Eliminated** – Lack of income diversity risk and tax rate risk.

THE GARCIAS' ASSETS AFTER PLANNING

Taxable bucket	$48,636
Tax-deferred bucket (IRA)	$250,080
Tax-free bucket (Roth IRA)	$307,107
Annual guaranteed tax-free income	$89,950

As you can see, I was able to get the Garcias' assets into the correct buckets for their retirement. They have six months of basic living expenses (inflation-adjusted). They have less than $500,000 in their tax-deferred bucket, and everything else is in their tax-free bucket, with far more tax-free income than they had available under their traditional plan.

WHAT RISKS WERE REDUCED OR ELIMINATED?

Social Security Risk – The Garcias will be able to maximize their benefits by waiting until age 70/66, and they will be able to re-allocate their income to where their Social Security will not be taxed once they get their Roth conversions done.

Tax Rate Risk – The Garcias will have no taxable income once Mr. Garcia turns 72 based upon the current plan. They are in the 0% tax bracket, which means even if taxes double, two times zero is still zero!

Longevity Risk – The Garcias can enjoy a long life because they have a guaranteed income that will never run out. Plus, the longer they live the better their financial situation gets, which is a strong motivator for trying to take care of yourself so you can live longer.

Sequence of Return Risk – The market can go up and down, and it will not have an impact on the Garcias daily lifestyle. Once they annuitize the annuity, the income is guaranteed, so the only assets they have at risk are what is left in the taxable bucket, tax-deferred bucket, and the Roth IRA. And these assets are not expected to be used for their daily lifestyle.

Withdrawal Rate Risk – The withdrawal rate has been set as part of the planning I did for the Garcias. Their new plan will allow them to get an above-average withdrawal rate from their retirement assets because of the other risks we have been able to eliminate.

Long-Term Care Risk – If Mr. and Mrs. Garcia have a long-term care event, they will be able to activate the chronic illness rider on their life insurance policies. This will allow them to access the death benefit early to help cover the cost of the long-term care event. Their annuity also will double the payments during a long-term care event.

Inflation Risk – Not only do the Garcias have inflation-adjusted Social Security, but their new plan also includes an annuity that is inflation-adjusted. Their annuity payments will increase throughout their retirement as the annuity value increases due to investment growth.

Medicare Risk – Mr. Garcia is happy with his Medicare Advantage Plan, but he now knows he needs to check it each year to make sure there are no changes to his coverage. If he does find changes that he is not happy with, he can consult with a broker to look for other alternatives.

Elder Abuse Risk – This risk has been reduced because there is a plan in place to cover the Garcias' financial needs through their retirement. Mrs. Garcia now has a plan to provide the income and structure she needs to maintain the lifestyle she has enjoyed, even if Mr. Garcia were to pass away early due to complications from a long-term care event.

Lack of Income Diversity Risk – It seems like a small thing, but by having four sources of tax-free income, the Garcias are in a great position to be able to continue to manage the financial risks facing their retirement.

STREAMS OF TAX-FREE INCOME

- Roth annuity
- Tax-deferred IRA and Roth IRA
- Social Security
- Indexed Universal Life Insurance Policy

These four various streams of tax-free income will allow the Garcias to deal with all the various financial risks I have covered in this book. The Roth annuity and Social Security will be what the Garcias live off each month, and the remaining assets can be used for shock or aspirational expenses.

STEP 6 – IMPLEMENT THE RISK-BASED RETIREMENT PLAN

As you can see from Carlos and Maria Garcia's case study, a risk-free retirement can happen, but it will not happen overnight or without work. This type of planning often takes five to ten years to get all the pieces moved to where they need to be on the chessboard. If you want our help, please go to www.retiremen-triskadvisors.com where you can get signed up for a risk-based retirement plan.